RAND

Federal Policy Options for Improving the Education of Low-Income Students

Volume I
Findings and Recommendations

Iris C. Rotberg
James J. Harvey

with Kelly E. Warner

Supported by the Lilly Endowment Inc.

INSTITUTE ON EDUCATION
AND TRAINING

RAND's Institute on Education and Training conducts policy analysis to help improve education and training for all Americans.

The Institute examines *all* forms of education and training that people may get during their lives. These include formal schooling from preschool through college; employer-provided training (civilian and military); postgraduate education; proprietary trade schools; and the informal learning that occurs in families, in communities, and with exposure to the media. Reexamining the field's most basic premises, the Institute goes beyond the narrow concerns of each component to view the education and training enterprise as a whole. It pays special attention to how the parts of the enterprise affect one another and how they are shaped by the larger environment. The Institute

- Examines the performance of the education and training system
- Analyzes problems and issues raised by economic, demographic, and national security trends
- Evaluates the impact of policies on broad, system-wide concerns
- Helps decisionmakers formulate and implement effective solutions.

To ensure that its research affects policy and practice, the Institute conducts outreach and disseminates findings to policymakers, educators, researchers, and the public. It also trains policy analysts in the field of education.

RAND is a private, nonprofit institution, incorporated in 1948, which engages in nonpartisan research and analysis on problems of national security and the public welfare. The Institute builds on RAND's long tradition—interdisciplinary, empirical research held to the highest standards of quality, objectivity, and independence.

PREFACE

The United States faces the difficult challenge of improving the education available to students from low-income families. Because family income, family educational level, and student educational achievement are closely correlated, low-income children, in effect, often face a double handicap: They have greater needs than more affluent children, but they attend schools with substantially smaller resources.

Based on these broad considerations, the RAND Institute on Education and Training, in consultation with the Committee on Education and Labor, U.S. House of Representatives, undertook an analysis of federal policy options to improve education in low-income areas. The analysis focuses on Chapter 1 of the Elementary and Secondary Education Act of 1965, the nation's $6.1 billion program for assisting disadvantaged students in primary and secondary schools. It draws on (1) a comprehensive review of existing evaluation data on Chapter 1, (2) invited commentaries by 91 policymakers, researchers, and educators (teachers, principals, and administrators) describing the strengths and shortcomings of Chapter 1, and (3) a commissioned study of federal options for school finance equalization.

The results of the analysis are reported in this three-volume study.

- *Federal Policy Options for Improving the Education of Low-Income Students,* Volume I, *Findings and Recommendations,* MR-209-LE, by Iris C. Rotberg and James J. Harvey, with Kelly E. Warner, assesses the current Chapter 1 program and describes a strategy for reformulating the program to encourage fundamental improvements in the quality of education available to low-income students.

- *Federal Policy Options for Improving the Education of Low-Income Students,* Volume II, *Commentaries,* MR-210-LE, by Iris C. Rotberg, editor, with Kelly E. Warner and Nancy Rizor, provides the texts of the invited papers.

- *Federal Policy Options for Improving the Education of Low-Income Students,* Volume III, *Countering Inequity in School Finance,* MR-211-LE, by Stephen M. Barro, assesses federal options for providing supplemental funding for the disadvantaged in the face of inequity in school finance.

The Lilly Endowment Inc. funded the research. The study was completed in spring 1993, in time for congressional deliberations on the reauthorization of Chapter 1.

Georges Vernez
Director, Institute on Education and Training

We must face everyday the realities of the unequal hand dealt to our children and to our schools.

Constance E. Clayton, Superintendent
Philadelphia Public Schools

CONTENTS

FIGURE

TABLES

SUMMARY

The RAND Institute on Education and Training, in consultation with the House of Representatives Committee on Education and Labor, undertook an analysis of federal policy options to improve education in low-income areas. The analysis focuses on Chapter 1 of the Elementary and Secondary Education Act of 1965, the nation's $6.1 billion program for assisting "disadvantaged" students in primary and secondary schools.[1]

The study considered a broad array of questions. For example, can Chapter 1, as currently financed, respond to recent increases in the incidence of poverty? What new possibilities for program improvement would emerge if federal funding for the education of disadvantaged students increased substantially? What are the consequences of alternative approaches for distributing funds and selecting students, and for increasing the level of resources available to low-income school districts? Can federal funds be used as an incentive to encourage greater school finance equalization? Is there any reason to believe that low-income students would benefit if the focus of Chapter 1 changed from supplemental services to "schoolwide improvement?" What are the effects of current Chapter 1 testing requirements?

Because of our changing societal conditions, we see an increasing need for more services to our disadvantaged students.

Nancy D. Booth, Teacher

This report, Volume I of the study, reviews the accomplishments of the Chapter 1 program, assesses its status today, and argues that it needs to be fundamentally reshaped to meet the challenges of tomorrow.

Background

The United States faces the difficult challenge of improving the education of students from low-income families. Because family income, family education level, and student educational achievement are closely correlated, low-income children often face a double handicap: They have greater needs than more affluent children, yet they attend schools with substantially fewer resources.

Chapter 1 is designed to do two things: (1) deliver federal funds to local school districts and schools responsible for the education of students from low-income families and (2) supplement the educational services provided in those districts to low-achieving students. School districts with ten or more children from families below the poverty level are eligible to receive Chapter 1 funds.

---

[1]See also Volume II, *Commentaries*, MR-210-LE, and Volume III, *Countering Inequity in School Finance*, MR-211-LE. The quotations in the margins of this volume are taken from the commentaries in Volume II. The respondents' titles refer to their responsibilities at the time the commentaries were written.

There cannot be meaningful excellence in education without a concern for equity.

Texas Education Agency Position Statement

Chapter 1 uses two separate formulas to distribute funds: the Basic Grant and a separate Concentration Grant. The Basic Grant provides money to the counties of each state, based on the number of low-income children and state per pupil expenditures. Where school district and county boundaries do not coincide, the state divides county allocations of Chapter 1 funds (as determined by the incidence of poverty) among the districts.

The Concentration Grant provides additional money (10 percent of Chapter 1 funds) to counties if at least 15 percent, or 6500, of the children aged 5 to 17 are from families with income below the poverty line. However, this grant has little concentrating effect; instead, it spreads a relatively small amount of money quite broadly.

School districts allocate funds to schools according to poverty and achievement. Schools select eligible students not on income criteria, but on the basis of "educational deprivation," normally determined by performance on standardized achievement tests or by teacher recommendations.

As a result, Chapter 1, for the most part, provides supplemental services to individually selected children within a school. Typically, funds are used for remedial reading and mathematics programs. Chapter 1 funds also support such programs as computer-assisted instruction, English as a second language, the teaching of reasoning and problem solving, early childhood activities, health and nutrition services, counseling and social services, and summer activities.

Chapter 1 provides essential supplemental services to large numbers of students nationwide. While it benefits many of these students, however, it has virtually no effect on overall school quality. It has not kept pace with the needs in either poor inner-city or poor rural schools. As designed, it cannot provide fundamental schoolwide improvements because (1) the amount of funding is small in relation to overall education expenditures and (2) the funds are widely dispersed. Further, because public school expenditures vary tremendously among states, districts in a state, and schools in a district, less money is devoted to the education of many Chapter 1 participants, even after the addition of Chapter 1 funds, than is devoted to the education of other children across the nation.

Indeed, Chapter 1's multiple purposes—an amalgamation aimed at assisting low-income districts while also providing funds for low-achieving children in wealthy districts—have produced a difficult combination of objectives: improving the overall quality of education in low-income communities while raising the achievement of the lowest-performing students in a large proportion of the nation's schools—all without sufficient resources.

Because funds are spread so broadly across states, districts, and schools, the neediest schools rarely have the resources to do much more than provide remedial basic skills programs. The funds certainly are not adequate to improve the quality of education generally—for poor children or for low-achieving children. In short, given the current level and distribution of resources, Chapter 1 cannot lead to comprehensive improvements in low-income communities.

Recommendations

The study recommends three basic changes:

1. Increase Chapter 1 funding for the nation's lowest-income school districts and schools.

The existing Chapter 1 funding mechanism spreads the available funds thinly and widely, taking little account of the disproportionate educational problems faced by school districts with high concentrations of poor children and the serious underfunding of their schools. Because of the high correlation between poverty and educational problems, children in poor schools need substantially more educational resources than do more affluent children, yet they receive much less. While school districts receive larger amounts of Chapter 1 funding as their *numbers* of low-income students increase, districts with high *concentrations* of low-income students do not receive larger allocations per poor pupil.

We must insist on programs of sufficient size, scope, and quality to achieve the desired outcomes.

Paul Weckstein, Co-Director, Education Center

The proposed changes would alter the distribution pattern by providing substantially greater aid per low-income child to the districts and schools with the most severe poverty-related problems. Chapter 1 funds would be concentrated by merging the present Basic Grant and Concentration Grant formulas into a single weighted formula that provides more money per poor child as the proportion of poor children in a district increases. Funds would be allocated to states, rather than to counties; states, in turn, would distribute the money under the new formula. Similar weighting could ensure that the funds went to the poorer schools in a school district.

Under the proposed formula, almost all districts currently eligible for Chapter 1 would continue to receive some funding. In practice, the level of funding in a district would depend on the combined effects of (1) the overall Chapter 1 appropriations and (2) the degree of weighting for low-income districts built into the formula. Because of the needs of low-income school districts, consideration should be given to the use of a formula weighted by concentration of poor children regardless of the overall level of Chapter 1 appropriations.

2. Reformulate Chapter 1 to encourage fundamental improvements in the quality of education available to low-income children of all achievement levels.

If sufficient Chapter 1 funding is available, the study proposes that the funds go to encourage schoolwide improvement for the broad range of low-income children in the designated schools. This change could dramatically improve educational opportunities for the most disadvantaged children. The purpose is to provide the poorer schools with the resources needed to make comprehensive changes in their educational offerings.

No group of students can be assisted in significant ways unless the school supports the needs of all students.

Henry M. Levin, Professor

A combination of poverty, immigration, a weak local economy, and program fragmentation have rendered many schools incapable of serving the majority of their students. We cannot argue either that students need "just a little extra," or that only a small minority of students suffers from selective neglect. Many of these students need help. Yet, Chapter 1 reaches relatively few of them, and only in narrow instructional areas. The point is that some schools are so pervasively inadequate and underfunded that they need basic reform, not the addition of a few services at the margin.

If the current, limited Chapter 1 resources went into a school's overall budget, however, many children now receiving special services would probably lose them, while the overall quality of the education program would not improve noticeably. It is hardly meaningful to recommend schoolwide projects in a school that receives only enough Chapter 1 money to support (as is often the case) one aide or a part-time teacher. If a school does not have sufficient resources, it would be better to let children continue to receive supplementary services.

3. Use a separate general aid program to provide incentives for equalizing overall funding within states.

The first two recommendations—increasing resources to the neediest communities and reformulating Chapter 1 to serve low-income children at all achievement levels—can lead to significant improvements in the quality of education in poor communities. By themselves, however, improvements in Chapter 1 cannot address a more fundamental problem in U.S. public education: the large disparities in expenditures across school districts.

One approach to these disparities is to use the Chapter 2 Block Grant program as the base for a system of fiscal incentives to encourage states to narrow the expenditure differential between rich and poor school districts. It appears feasible, with available data, to assess both the potential effectiveness of incentives for equity and the likely distribution of the proposed incentive grants among states.

The study strongly recommends against using Chapter 1 for this purpose. First, some states would be forced to turn down the Chapter 1 funds because they did not have the resources to increase expenditures to poor districts. Second, Chapter 1 participants, already harmed by unevenly distributed education expenditures, would be further harmed if federal funds were withdrawn.

Program Accountability and Achievement Testing

This report calls for fundamental changes in the delivery of federal education services. The proposed strategy involves substantially increasing funding for the nation's lowest-income districts and schools, thereby facilitating the adoption of schoolwide projects focused on enriching the educational experience of low-income children of all achievement levels. These changes will require a new concept of accountability in Chapter 1.

Until now, two distinct approaches have characterized program accountability. The first approach involved national evaluations of Chapter 1, as well as studies that provided a more general sense of trends in the education of low-income students. The general studies included information about (1) resources and educational programs in low-income schools and (2) student attainment, including test scores, grades, promotion rates, attendance rates, high school graduation, and college attendance. The best of these studies have served the education community well in the past and can be expected to continue to provide essential information about both the effectiveness of Chapter 1 and, more generally, trends in the education of low-income students.

The second approach consisted of annual programs of achievement testing at the local level for purposes of accountability. For reasons described below, the study concludes that this approach has had adverse consequences and should be replaced by accountability methods that are more consistent with the reformulation of Chapter 1 recommended in this report.

Standardized tests tell us what we already know, frustrate the students, and painfully remind them of their failure.

Joan Stoltz, Teacher

Chapter 1 testing of students currently permeates virtually every aspect of the program. Students are tested first to determine program eligibility and, at the end of the year, to see how much they have learned. Policymakers hope that the more they hold schools accountable for the test scores of Chapter 1 students, the more their educational programs will improve. Instead, the proliferation of testing has led to a diverse set of problems and negative incentives:

- The testing encourages the teaching of a narrow set of measurable skills. The mandated tests—and the rote learning associated with them—are particularly common in classrooms with high proportions of low-income and minority children.

- The use of test scores for funds allocation typically results in less funding for the schools that make achievement gains. The reliance on test scores, therefore, works against schools that have strong programs in the early years or promote successful students out of Chapter 1. If they succeed, as defined by the test scores, they lose money.

- The quality of an education system, of an individual school, or of a specific program—for example, Chapter 1—cannot be measured simply by comparing test score fluctuations from one year to another, or by comparing schools or classrooms on test scores. The reason is that the results do not control for changes in student population, incentives for encouraging certain students to take (or not to take) the test, or the consistency, or lack of it, between the test and the instructional program.

The current Chapter 1 testing requirements do not lead to improvements in education. They tell us only what we already know—the effects of inadequate resources and poverty on the learning experience.

What is tested is what is taught.

John Ellis, Chief State School Officer

The evidence from both research and practical experience suggests that federal testing requirements do not lead to improvements in education. This conclusion also applies to recent proposals to increase Chapter 1 accountability requirements as a trade-off for reducing other regulations. The fact is that these proposals cannot be implemented without continuing to incur the negative consequences of current testing practices.

The study recommends, therefore, that federal requirements for Chapter 1 testing—either for purposes of accountability or for determining student or school eligibility for program participation—be eliminated. Chapter 1 students should take the same tests routinely given to other children in their school district. Federal testing requirements would cease to influence the educational program in low-income schools, to encourage the teaching of a narrow set of skills, and to create perverse incentives that punish schools for raising achievement.

Instead of federal requirements for Chapter 1 testing, a system is needed to encourage accountability at the local level. The study proposes revising the program improvement concept to encompass far broader measures. These might include (1) indicators of student performance and progress, for example, grades, attendance, promotions, and dropout rates; and (2) information about the school's educational program as shown, for example, by course offerings, class size, and teacher qualifications. Chapter 1 schools could provide this information to district officials, who would, in turn, report to state Chapter 1 officials. The choice of specific measures should be left to the discretion of states and localities, which have the best information about both the availability of data and the measures that would most closely reflect a district's educational program.

This approach, combined with national studies and evaluations, would provide valuable information to all involved with Chapter 1: Federal policymakers could draw on the results of national evaluations to gauge the effectiveness of the national effort; elected federal officials would be alerted to significant progress or problems in schools in their own constituencies; state officials would have statewide access to district reports; school district officials would have much richer information on operations in their own Chapter 1 schools and the problems that these schools face; and parents and community leaders would be able to judge how well their local schools were doing.

Improving the Education of Low-Income Children

Despite the growing severity of the problems Chapter 1 was designed to address, the program has not been modified to respond to the realities of increased poverty and vast differences in educational expenditures between rich and poor school districts.

- The first issue is financial: Schools serving many low-income students need more resources.
- The second is a matter of focus: Federal funds should be directed to the areas with the largest concentration of these youngsters.
- The third issue involves educational and policy coherence: If sufficient resources are available, Chapter 1 can play a much more significant role in improving education in our poorest communities by encouraging schoolwide improvement.

The environment for Chapter 1 today is far more challenging than the problems for which the program was originally designed. The numbers of poor children and the problems in high-poverty schools have increased substantially. In recent years, several "reforms"—restructured schools, vouchers, national standards, and national testing—have been proposed to strengthen the nation's education system. Neither individually nor collectively do they respond to the problems of low-income schools.

Schools whose Chapter 1 programs are not showing positive results are also demonstrating problems schoolwide.

Ed Obie, State Chapter 1 Director

Up until now, the nation has chosen not to make the needed investment in low-income schools. Under the circumstances, policymakers should be realistic about what can and cannot be accomplished by rhetoric about world-class standards, accountability, or choice. Setting vague and unrealistic goals, or constructing additional tests, does not substitute for high quality education. We will not produce better schools—no matter what peripheral reforms are implemented—unless we address the serious underfunding of education in poor communities. Further delays will result in diminished opportunities for this generation of low-income children.

ACKNOWLEDGMENTS

We are grateful to the many people who contributed to this report. The invited commentaries we received from educators, policymakers, and researchers nationwide provided invaluable information, from diverse perspectives, about the Chapter 1 program and related educational issues. The commentaries are a major source of the findings and recommendations of the study.

We are also indebted to a large number of other people who made major intellectual contributions to this report in interviews, meetings, and conversations. The observations of these colleagues—teachers, principals, counselors, school administrators, association representatives, government officials, researchers—continually remind us of the complexity of the issues involved in making recommendations for educational reform and of the risks in seeking simplistic solutions.

We wish to thank Stephen M. Barro of SMB Economic Research, Inc., for his major contributions to the school finance analysis in the report. Several colleagues at RAND made significant contributions to the study. We are grateful to Georges Vernez, Director of the RAND Institute on Education and Training, for his support and intellectual contributions throughout the research. We thank the following other RAND colleagues: Paul T. Hill made important contributions in areas of school reform and accountability; Nancy Rizor managed the process of inviting and organizing the commentaries and assisted in the general conduct of the study, with a high level of knowledge and judgment; and Donald P. Henry contributed meticulous and creative data analyses.

We also wish to thank Frank Harvey of James Harvey and Associates for his great skill and patience in producing innumerable early drafts of the manuscript.

Many colleagues in school systems, education associations, research institutions, and government gave generously of their time in providing data and other information pertaining to the study. Daphne Hardcastle, U.S. Department of Education, provided research findings on a wide range of topics throughout the course of the study. *Voices from the Field*, a report of Youth and America's Future (the William T. Grant Foundation Commission on Work, Family and Citizenship and the Institute for Educational Leadership), served as a model for the invited commentaries.

During the past year, there have been a number of other studies of the Chapter 1 program, including those by the U.S. Department of Education, the National Assessment of Chapter 1 Independent Review Panel, and the Commission on Chapter 1. Colleagues participating in these studies have been extremely helpful in sharing their findings and views on the program.

We wish to thank Lorraine M. McDonnell of the University of California Santa Barbara and Margot A. Schenet of the Congressional Research Service for their particularly valuable and thoughtful reviews. Finally, we are grateful to staff of the House Committee on Education and Labor for sharing with us their extensive knowledge and insights about the program and to the Lilly Endowment for making the study possible.

The views and recommendations presented in the report are solely those of the authors.

1. INTRODUCTION

Americans have traditionally viewed schools as the route to upward mobility. Grounded in deeply held beliefs about the nature of a just society, Americans began with the conviction that education is a good thing and that more of it is even better. Enrollment figures alone indicate the significance Americans attach to schooling. About 60 million people—more than one in four persons in the United States—are enrolled in a school, college or university, full or part time.[1]

The education system in the United States has served the needs of society quite well in this century. The uproar of the past decade about American education revolves largely around whether schools can continue to do so in the next century.

The national belief in education has coexisted with an equally powerful tradition that elementary and secondary education is a local responsibility, an area in which the national government should tread carefully, if at all. The tradition of local control meant that the first successful attempt to enact federal aid to schools, the National Defense Education Act of 1958, had to pass under the unassailable federal banner of national security. And, until the last generation, educational problems of low-income youngsters isolated in urban and remote rural pockets of poverty, attending poorly funded schools, rarely entered the dialogue about education.

All of that changed quite dramatically in 1965, when the federal government passed the Elementary and Secondary Education Act (ESEA). Title I of the Act constituted a major program for the education of "disadvantaged" students. Now in its 27th year, Title I—renamed Chapter 1 in 1981 by the Education Consolidation and Improvement Act (ECIA)—was the first federal education program to reach out and include the dispossessed, based on the almost universal belief that education is the road to success for individuals and the larger society.

The enactment of the program was a significant event, not simply in the nation's educational progress but in the nation's larger agenda as well. It signaled a renewed commitment to equality of opportunity and to the right of low-income and minority youngsters to claim a place in the American future. It was an impressive signal.

The accomplishments of the program have been equally impressive. In scale, reach, and stability, Chapter 1 stands head and shoulders above

Chapter 1 is the best federal education program in existence for meeting the needs of economically and educationally deprived children.

Lynn Beckwith, Jr., State and Federal Program Director

An overriding strength of Chapter 1 is its effect on the self-esteem of children who begin to experience success.

Margaret M. Baldwin, Teacher

---

[1]The quotations in the margins of this volume are taken from Volume II, *Commentaries*, MR-210-LE. The respondents' titles refer to their responsibilities at the time the commentaries were written.

every other program of federal assistance for elementary and secondary education:

- Between 1965 and 1991, Title I/Chapter 1 provided more than $70 billion for educational services that were provided in almost all of the nation's school districts and in large numbers of its schools.

- Each school year since 1965, between 4.4 and 5.1 million students (around 10 percent of enrollments) benefited from Chapter 1. While most Chapter 1 students are enrolled in public schools, 3.9 percent receive services in private schools, including church-related schools.

- Each year, Chapter 1 supports more than 62,000 full-time equivalent teachers, along with more than 67,000 full-time equivalent teachers' aides.

Ensure that all eligible nonpublic school students receive the services to which they are entitled.

Frederick H. Brigham, Jr., Executive Assistant, Education Association

In short, Chapter 1 has served millions of students and thousands of school districts and schools. It focuses the attention of educators on the needs of disadvantaged students. It offers extra dollars that, at the margin, permit financially strapped schools to assist poor and disadvantaged students. It provides students with supplemental basic skills instruction and, more recently, help in developing advanced skills. It encourages the evaluation of education practice.

Although it benefits many children, however, Chapter 1 affects the overall quality of education in low-income communities only marginally. American education today faces the challenge of improving the program without in the process weakening its benefits to participating children.

This report reviews the Chapter 1 program's accomplishments, assesses its status today, and argues that it needs to be fundamentally reshaped to meet the challenges of tomorrow. The report draws on a comprehensive review of existing data on Chapter 1 and a specially commissioned study of federal options for school finance equalization.

It also draws on invited commentaries by 91 respondents—policymakers, researchers, and educators—describing the strengths and shortcomings of Chapter 1 and recommending changes that might increase its effectiveness. The commentaries, while not a representative sample, were selected to represent diverse constituencies and perspectives. Requests for commentary were sent to over 400 potential respondents: state administrators in all 50 states and the District of Columbia; a wide range of school district administrators, teachers, and principals; key education association officials; and a broad representation of researchers and policy analysts.

The commentaries submitted reflect the diversity built into the initial list. They include 16 from state administrators (chief state school officers and Chapter 1 coordinators), 18 from district administrators (school superintendents and Chapter 1 coordinators), 18 from school personnel, 13 from association representatives, and 26 from researchers and policy analysts.[2]

The commentaries offer in-depth analyses of the issues discussed in this report, as well as of topics, for example, private schools, vouchers, and state administration, that go beyond the scope of the study. While the respondents' conclusions reflect the diversity of the sample, they also focus on the key issues analyzed in this report.

First, there is wide agreement among the commentaries about the need to increase the level and concentration of Chapter 1 funds. This recommendation is made in the context of the growing needs of low-income school districts resulting from increases in poverty, societal problems, fiscal crises, unemployment, and immigration.

Chapter 1 should provide coverage for all eligible youngsters. The Chapter 1 funds [should be] made available in the form of a voucher or scholarship.

Denis P. Doyle, Senior Fellow, Research Organization

Second, the commentaries discuss the need to coordinate Chapter 1 more fully with the child's overall educational experience. They argue that Chapter 1 cannot be separated from the general quality of the school or, indeed, from the problems of poverty in the broader environment. Many respondents recommend that Chapter 1 funds be used for schoolwide improvement rather than focusing services primarily on remedial instruction for selected groups of students. Suggestions also are made for coordinating Chapter 1 more fully with other categorical programs, as well as with health and social services.

However, not all respondents are sanguine about fully integrating Chapter 1 with other programs. Some argue for the continuation of supplemental programs, noting the benefits of "preventive" reading and mathematics programs, remedial programs, or programs that focus on reasoning and problem solving, some of which may work best when children are taught in small groups apart from the regular classroom.

Commentaries also note potential negative consequences of folding Chapter 1 into the broader program, for example: (1) insufficient funds to make the proposed changes a viable option, (2) the risk that Chapter 1 funds would be used as general aid if the focus on individual students were eliminated, and (3) a channeling of funds away from Chapter 1 if it were combined with other categorical programs without at the same time providing a consistent federal framework across programs.

Third, the commentaries point to a wide range of problems related to current Chapter 1 testing requirements. Respondents argue that the requirements (1) encourage an emphasis on rote learning at the expense of higher order cognitive skills, (2) result in less funding for schools that make achievement gains, and (3) often do not provide the type of information that is useful either for accountability or for program improvement. Some of the commentaries accept the premise on which current testing requirements are based; their recommended changes are intended

---

[2]Volume II of this report, *Commentaries*, MR-210-LE, presents the complete papers.

to improve the operation of these requirements. Others question more fundamental aspects of the requirements and argue that the system as a whole should be reformulated.

Chapter 1 must take the lead in making use of new and innovative instructional programs.

Richard M. Long, Government Relations Specialist, Education Association

Sections 2 and 3 of the report present the core of the argument: whether Chapter 1 as currently funded and structured accomplishes the objectives defined and periodically reaffirmed since 1965. Section 2 introduces Chapter 1 and describes changes in the larger educational environment since the program was enacted in 1965, focusing on the growth of poverty in many schools. It asks whether federal compensatory education efforts provide adequate resources to accomplish national goals. It also assesses trends in school finance and differences in the quality of education offered in low-income and upper-income neighborhoods. Section 3 takes up the issue of the services provided under Chapter 1 and the likelihood that they can have any appreciable long-term effects on the quality of education available to low-income students.

Section 4 suggests the need for a new three-part federal strategy including (1) a substantial increase in Chapter 1 funding for the nation's lowest-income school districts and schools; (2) the reformulation of Chapter 1 to encourage fundamental improvements in the quality of education available to low-income children of all achievement levels; and (3) a separate general aid program to provide incentives for equalizing overall funding within states.

Section 5 addresses issues of evaluation and accountability and examines the growth of achievement testing spawned by Chapter 1 to determine whether it has improved education generally, or Chapter 1 in particular. The final section argues that myths about educational performance in low-income areas have blocked effective federal action and that it is time to move beyond these misconceptions to act on the national need, first identified in 1965, for effective education for every child.

2. COMPENSATORY EDUCATION AND SCHOOL FINANCE

Chapter 1 is designed to do two things: (1) deliver federal funds to local school districts and schools responsible for the education of students from low-income families and (2) supplement the educational services provided in those districts to low-achieving students. School districts with ten or more children from families below the poverty level are eligible to receive Chapter 1 funds.

The central strength of Chapter 1 is the focus of service for educationally disadvantaged children.

Robert R. Spillane, Superintendent of Schools

Funding is directed by a formula that provides funds to counties within each state, based on counts of low-income children and state per pupil expenditures. Where school district and county boundaries do not coincide, the state divides county allocations of Chapter 1 funds (as determined by the incidence of poverty) among the districts. School districts then allocate funds to schools based on poverty and achievement criteria.

Schools, in turn, select eligible students not on income criteria, but on the basis of "educational deprivation," normally determined by performance on standardized achievement tests or by teacher recommendations. As a result, Chapter 1, for the most part, provides supplemental services to individually selected children within a school.

Evolution of Chapter 1

Although Chapter 1 was enacted in 1965 as part of a broad assault on poverty in the United States, the statute's ambiguous language led many initially to believe that funds could be used as general aid to education. Since 1965, the program has been modified many times to clarify legislative intent, respond to evaluation findings, and react to broader national concerns about education. For example, the 1970 amendments responded to critical evaluations by requiring that Chapter 1 funds—the program was then known as Title I—be used to "supplement not supplant" state and local support, i.e., add to local education funding, not replace it. The 1970 amendments also required that Chapter 1 schools receive state and local funding "comparable" to support for other schools in the same district, before the addition of Chapter 1 resources.

Change for the sake of change does not guarantee improvement in services.

Art Kono, District Chapter 1 Director

Legislation of 1974 required parent advisory councils (PACs) at the school and district levels. In 1978, Congress strengthened the PAC requirements, added a new concentration grant program for school districts with many low-income youngsters, specified how districts should rank schools for inclusion in the program, authorized state agencies to review local programs, and permitted "schoolwide" projects in schools with 75 percent or more low-income students, provided the district matched federal funds in these schools.

The Reagan administration deregulated education funding in 1981 through the Education Consolidation and Improvement Act. Title I was renamed Chapter 1, and the regulatory framework governing comparability, school selection, state monitoring, and parent involvement was relaxed.

The student with the most need may receive the most fragmented instruction.

James P. Comer, Professor

Finally, the 1988 Hawkins-Stafford amendments added significant new features that encouraged program coordination with other school offerings, expanded Chapter 1's horizons from basic skills to the advanced skills, dropped local matching requirements for schoolwide projects, and required states to mount "program improvement" efforts permitting district and state intervention to help troubled schools. In brief, Title I/Chapter 1 has grown and evolved over a quarter century into a complicated program interacting with virtually every aspect of state and local education finance, administration, and education services.

Chapter 1 and a Changing Society

Societal changes have more than matched the growth and evolution of Chapter 1. Since Chapter 1 was first enacted, the number of children in poverty has grown. The proportion of the American population from minority backgrounds has increased, and with it the minority youth population. Despite the development of a large and growing minority middle class in recent decades, many minority Americans continue to live in a cycle of joblessness and poverty.

Children in Poverty

Growing numbers of Chapter 1 children are overwhelmed by social, health, and economic problems —problems that profoundly influence their capacity to succeed in school.

Michael D. Usdan, President of Research Organization

As the United States moves toward the 21st century, more low-income children are showing up at the schoolhouse door. Chapter 1 was enacted at a time of growing optimism that poverty could be virtually eliminated in this country. In fact, the percentage of all children below the poverty level dropped from 26.5 percent in 1960 to a low of 14.9 percent in 1970 (National Center for Education Statistics, June 1992). The percentage increased during the 1980s, however, reaching 19.9 percent in 1990—almost where it had been in 1965, the year in which Chapter 1 was enacted.

From 1980 through 1990, one in five children under the age of 18 was living in poverty. Although a far larger *proportion* of minority children than white children are poor, a large number of poor children come from the majority Anglo population: In 1991, almost 8.3 million white children lived in poverty, compared with 4.6 million African-American and 2.9 million Hispanic children (U.S. Bureau of the Census, 1992).

Minority Youth

Perhaps the most striking demographic trend lies in the makeup of the American youth population. Thirty percent of all public school students today are members of a minority group: African-American, Native American, Eskimo or Aleut, Asian or Pacific Islander, or Hispanic. In 35 of the 45 largest urban school districts, minority enrollments outnumber nonminority enrollments. On average, the enrollment in the 45 districts is about 70 percent minority (Council of Great City Schools, 1988).

Although urban areas have been in economic trouble for 20 years or more, enrollments in many big city schools have been increasing since the mid-1980s as a result of immigration. In recent years, New York, Los Angeles, Chicago, and Miami together have enrolled nearly 100,000 new students each year who are either foreign born or children of immigrants (Hill, 1992). These students need intensified services.

According to these demographic trends, the proportion of public school enrollments of minority students nationwide will reach nearly 40 percent by 2010 (Hodgkinson, 1989). Census estimates indicate that the total youth population will grow very slowly through 2010, by about .5 percent. But the small total change in the youth population involves a decrease of 3.8 million in the number of white youth combined with an increase of 4.4 million in the number of minority youth. Many of these children live below the poverty line: By 1991, 45.6 percent of African-American and 39.8 percent of Hispanic children were officially poor (U.S. Bureau of the Census, 1992). Chapter 1 must respond to these developments.

Changes in the economic base of many urban communities have resulted in declines in employment opportunities, depressed wages and high poverty rates.

Carolyn D. Herrington, Professor, and E. Juliana Paré, Research Assistant

Student Needs

The large numbers of low-income students pose special problems for American schools. Bleak, crime-ridden inner-city neighborhoods with widespread unemployment and large low-income minority populations receive a lot of national attention. The problems of rural poverty—often involving poorly educated parents trying to make ends meet while isolated, unemployed, and without health insurance—are less well known, but equally severe. Thirty percent of children in central cities live below the poverty line. Twenty-two percent of children living in rural areas are poor; moreover, these areas contain some of the most severely impoverished communities in the nation—in Appalachian Kentucky, on Sioux Indian reservations in South Dakota, along the Mexican border in Texas, and in the Mississippi River delta. In many counties, more than half of all children are poor (Johnson et al., 1991).

We tend to associate concentrations of low-income children with depressed inner-city areas, but children living on remote Indian reservations or in economically blighted regions have comparable needs.

Jay K. Donaldson, State Chapter 1 Director

The schools in these areas often do not have the financial resources needed to provide even a minimally adequate educational program for these children. At the same time, high-quality education has been ceaselessly sold as the solution to the nation's economic problems. In this environment, the resources devoted to the educational needs of poor youngsters should have increased significantly throughout the 1980s. Unfortunately, while the number of low-income students increased in the last decade, and many of these youngsters bring severe problems with them to school, the resources have not matched the growing need.

Delivering Federal Funds

Given the present level of resources, we may be asking schools to achieve the unachievable.

Thomas B. Timar, Professor

Chapter 1 grants are designed to provide supplemental educational services to participating children. They are based on the premise that extra, federally funded services will compensate, at least in part, for the impediments to learning associated with living in low-income communities (hence the term *compensatory education*) and, therefore, gaps in educational performance between low-income and more advantaged children will be reduced. As a matter of simple logic, it is unrealistic to expect Chapter 1 to close the learning gap if it does not translate into higher per pupil expenditures—and hence more educational resources and services—to participants than to the general pupil population.

We discuss below whether Chapter 1 as currently funded provides adequate resources to make significant improvements in the education of low-income students.

The Contribution of Chapter 1

Chapter 1 is simply one small part of a complex system of intergovernmental school finance. Prior to 1965, local school districts provided over two-thirds of school funding and the states most of the rest. The federal government was hardly involved. Today, the national average indicates that states and localities share school finance obligations almost equally: states, 47.2 percent in 1989–1990; localities, 46.6 percent (National Center for Education Statistics, October 1992). The national average includes wide state-by-state differences. Hawaii and New Hampshire are the outlier states: Hawaii provided 87 percent of the financing of local schools in 1988–1989; New Hampshire, 8.5 percent.

The federal government's contribution is about 6 percent of the revenues for elementary and secondary schools, a proportion that includes both Chapter 1 and other programs, such as bilingual education, special and vocational education, and impact aid—most of them distributed largely without regard to school district wealth or the number of children in poverty. Two considerations flow from this pattern of school finance: First, the federal contribution is only a small portion of the support provided by states and localities; second, this contribution is delivered in the context of widely differing funding patterns among states.

In terms of funding for local school districts, Chapter 1 contains two separate formulas: the Basic Grant and a separate Concentration Grant, both based on county counts of low-income children. Any school district with ten or more low-income children is eligible to receive a Chapter 1 grant. Except for some relatively minor changes in the Concentration Grant program and the data bases that drive the program, the federal formula has gone unchanged since 1974.

The following key considerations bear on the allocation of Chapter 1 funds:[1]

- Although the federal government sends checks to states, it actually distributes funds by county. A state's allocation is the sum of the allocations to all its counties.

- Basic Grants (90 percent of all Chapter 1 funds) are allocated in proportion to the number of eligible poor children aged 5 to 17 in a *county* (based mainly on the number of children from families with income below the poverty line, as reported in the decennial census), adjusted by a *state* per pupil expenditure factor, defined as state expenditure per pupil but not less than 80 percent nor more than 120 percent of national average expenditure per pupil.

- Counties also receive Concentration Grants (10 percent of Chapter 1 funds) if at least 15 percent, or 6500, of the children aged 5 to 17 are from families with income below the poverty line.

- States distribute Chapter 1 funds to school districts in each county, if necessary, in proportion to a state-selected indicator of the number of low-income children in each district.

In general, the state per pupil expenditure provisions are a seriously flawed proxy for local education costs:

> Specifically, the per pupil expenditure factor in the formula gives high-spending states up to 50 percent more federal aid than low-spending states per low-income child. The standard rationale for the per pupil expenditure factor is that it adjusts for interstate differentials in the cost of education. [But,] . . . per pupil expenditure is not a satisfactory proxy for the cost of education. It exaggerates cost differentials among the states, giving the high-spending states more federal aid and the low-spending states less federal aid than would a valid cost adjustment.[2]

Chapter 1 funds clearly do not compensate for differences in education spending among states:

> Even without the per pupil expenditure factor, the interstate distribution would, at best, be neutral. Chapter 1 funds would not be distributed in a manner that reduces or compensates for interstate disparities in spending. With the per pupil expenditure factor, the federal formula exacerbates fiscal inequity by giving more compensatory education dollars per poor pupil to the already high-spending states.[3]

---

[1]See Volume III of this study, *Countering Inequity in School Finance*, MR-211-LE, and Barro (1991).

[2] See Volume III of this study.

[3]Ibid.

Counties and school districts receive larger amounts of Chapter 1 funding as their *numbers* of low-income students increase, but counties and districts with high *concentrations* of low-income students do not receive larger allocations per poor pupil. Moreover, because Chapter 1 funds are available to any district with ten or more eligible children, the funds are spread very broadly.

Almost every district receives [Chapter 1] funds. This dilutes the effect in the most poverty-ridden districts.

Deborah M. McGriff, School Superintendent

Chapter 1 funds go to 90 percent of the nation's school districts (only very small districts or districts that do not want Chapter 1 programs are excluded); districts, in turn, enjoy wide latitude in defining the universe of eligible schools. Approximately 71 percent of elementary schools and 39 percent of secondary schools receive Chapter 1 funds. Almost half of the elementary schools with fewer than 10 percent poor children in their student body receive Chapter 1 funds (U. S. Department of Education, 1992).

Although the 1988 Hawkins-Stafford amendments modified the Concentration Grant formula (by lowering county poverty thresholds from either 20 percent or 5000 low-income children to 15 percent or 6500), the broad distribution of Chapter 1 funds has changed little since 1984 (U. S. Department of Education, 1992). Forty-five percent of all Chapter 1 students in 1984–1985 lived in districts in the highest-poverty quartile. Five years later, the percentage was unchanged. In 1984–1985, 9 percent of all public school Chapter 1 students lived in relatively affluent districts (poverty levels below 7.2 percent); by 1990–1991, the proportion had risen slightly to 11 percent. Thus, despite changes in the Concentration Grant formula, a slightly larger proportion of Chapter 1 students lived in more affluent districts.

Trends in Federal Spending

The increased levels of funding, as well as the increased flexibility in providing services to eligible students, have been beneficial.

John Hooper, State Chapter 1 Director

Federal spending on Chapter 1 appears to have grown handsomely since the program first began. Between 1966 and 1992, funding for Chapter 1 increased almost sixfold in *current* dollars, from $959 million in the first year of operation to $6.1 billion currently. Even during the 1980s, a period of particularly difficult budget constraints, Chapter 1 funding in current dollars nearly doubled, from $2.6 billion in 1980 to $4.4 billion in 1990.

Current appropriations are deceptive, however. The critical issue for Chapter 1 is whether real spending in *constant* dollars is increasing and whether Chapter 1 is responding to increases in the low-income population and to the severe new needs these youngsters bring with them to school.

Figure 1 demonstrates the funding trends for the Chapter 1 program. During most of the 1980s, funding was essentially flat in terms of the buying power of Chapter 1 appropriations. One of the lowest points for the program in constant funding occurred in 1983, the year the federal government proclaimed that a "rising tide of mediocrity" in American schools put the nation's future at risk (National Commission on Excellence in Education, 1983). During the past few years, Chapter 1 funding has increased substantially and has exceeded the inflation rate.

However, Chapter 1 was never funded at a high enough level to address the needs of low-income schools; moreover, Chapter 1 resources are widely dispersed. Thus, even with the recent funding increases, Chapter 1 cannot respond to the growing educational crisis in low-income areas.

These cold numbers translate into large numbers of real children who live in poverty, but who are not served because of insufficient resources.

Thomas Sobol, Chief State School Officer

Providing Supplementary Services

Although Chapter 1 funds are supposed to buy supplemental services for disadvantaged students, the wide variation in spending levels among states and localities, both among and within states, calls into question the supplemental character of Chapter 1. The education of Chapter 1 partic-

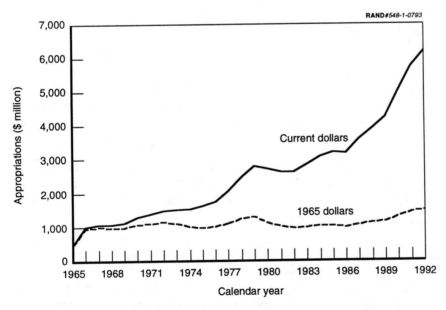

SOURCES: U.S. Department of Education (unpublished notes) and *Economic Report of the President, 1993*.

NOTE: To obtain calendar year appropriations, fiscal year appropriations were allocated to the year in which they fell.

Figure 1—Chapter 1 Appropriations in Current and Constant 1965 Dollars

*There are consider-
ably more students
in need of supple-
mentary services
than there are funds
to provide these
services.*

Milton D. Matthews,
State Compensatory
Education Director

ipants is often less well funded, federal aid notwithstanding, than that of other children in nearby communities and across the nation.[4]

States have no obligation under the legal framework to compensate for, or even consider, differences in per pupil expenditure across school district lines: A school in one district may receive, for example, $800 per Chapter 1 pupil in Chapter 1 funds plus $4000 in state and local funds, while non-Chapter 1 children in a neighboring district may receive $6000 in state- and locally-funded services. Likewise, at the national level, no federal rule is violated if one state's regular students receive more educational services than another state's Chapter 1 pupils.

Supplementation may be thought of on three levels. Narrow, local supplementation would be based on whether participating children received services that supplemented the services that other children in their school district received. A broader and more demanding standard would seek state-level supplementation, based on the degree to which participating children received more services than other children in their state. The broadest and most demanding standard would seek national supplementation, based on providing Chapter 1 participants with more services than other children throughout the nation.

Local Supplementation

Chapter 1 was designed to supplement only in the local sense. It was never intended to equalize educational expenditures within states, let alone across states. According to the statute and regulations, each school district receiving Chapter 1 funds must provide to its Chapter 1 pupils more resources and services than they would have received in the absence of Chapter 1.

The current Chapter 1 program includes requirements designed to ensure that the federal funds result in *additional* resources to districts, schools, and students (U.S. House of Representatives, 1991). Three regulations are especially important in this regard:

- The maintenance-of-effort provision, which applies to district-level expenditures, requires that either the combined fiscal effort per student or the aggregate expenditures of the district and the state for education for the preceding year be no less than 90 percent of the amount for the year before that.

- A second provision, which applies at the school level to the services provided by state and local funds, requires that the level of services in Chapter 1 schools be at least comparable to those in non-Chapter 1 schools before the addition of compensatory funds. A district is

---

[4]The discussion of Chapter 1 supplementation in this section is drawn in part from Volume III of this study.

considered to have met the requirements if it has filed with the state a written assurance that it has established and implemented (1) a districtwide salary schedule; (2) a policy to ensure equivalence among schools in teachers, administrators, and auxiliary personnel; and (3) a policy to ensure equivalence among schools in the provision of curriculum materials and instructional supplies.

- A third requirement to supplement, not supplant, applies at the student level; it requires that Chapter 1 funds be used to provide supplemental programs for the education of children participating in Chapter 1.

State and National Supplementation

The wide variation in levels of regular state and local education spending, both among and within states, calls into question the supplemental character of Chapter 1 for children in the lower-spending jurisdictions. It would not matter so much that Chapter 1 is designed to supplement only by local standards if individuals competed academically and economically only within their own local communities, but that is obviously not the case.

The United States is a national economy, not a collection of isolated state and local economies. Children in Pike County, Kentucky (per pupil expenditures in 1989–1990 of $2600), need to be prepared to compete in the labor market not only against children from Jefferson County, Kentucky ($3900 per pupil), but also against children from Montgomery County, Maryland ($7300 per pupil).[5] Therefore, supplementation only in the narrow, local sense falls far short of the proclaimed goal of federal compensatory education policy, which is to put disadvantaged children throughout the United States on a more equal footing with their more advantaged peers.

Poor children need to learn about "making it" both where they are and in a larger world.

Robert D. Crangle, Attorney

As Table 1 indicates, wealthy districts across the country often outspend their poorer neighbors in the same state by 250–300 percent.

Public schools have relied on locally raised property taxes for a substantial share of their revenues. Despite court challenges to intrastate inequities in the financial support available to children, property taxes—which virtually guarantee these inequities—remain an important source of school finance. For example:

- The 300,000 students in the poorest Texas schools are supported with less than 3 percent of the state's property wealth, while the 300,000

---

[5] The cited expenditure figures are rounded off from data for 1989–1990 presented in U.S. Bureau of the Census (1992). See Volume III of this study.

Table 1

EXPENDITURE INEQUITY AMONG SCHOOL DISTRICTS IN SELECTED
STATES

State	School District Type	Expenditure Ratio
Illinois	Elementary	3.1 to 1
Michigan	Unified	2.3 to 1
New Jersey	Elementary	2.4 to 1
New York	Unified	2.6 to 1
Ohio	Unified	2.8 to 1
Pennsylvania	Unified	2.4 to 1
Texas	Unified	2.8 to 1

SOURCE: William Taylor and Dianne M. Piché, *Shortchanging Children: The Impact of Fiscal Inequity on the Education of Students at Risk*. Report prepared for the Committee on Education and Labor, U.S. House of Representatives, Serial No. 102.O, Washington, D.C.: U.S. Government Printing Office, 1991.

students in the wealthiest schools have over 25 percent of the state's property wealth behind them.

- The 100 poorest districts in Texas spend an average of $2978 per student, while the 100 wealthiest districts spent an average of $7233.

- Illinois school districts spend between $2356 and $8286 per student.

- In Mississippi, Pontotoc County schools spent only $1324 per child in 1986–1987, compared with $4018 in Claiborne County, the highest-spending district (William L. Taylor and Dianne M. Piché, 1991).

But even the children in the poorest districts in Texas and Illinois received a better deal than children in Pontotoc County, Mississippi. Indeed, some states spend twice as much per pupil, on average, than other states—even after adjusting for cost differentials. In the lowest-spending states, considerably less is spent on all students, advantaged and disadvantaged alike. Thus, instead of receiving extra resources that might help them catch up, many Chapter 1 pupils in lower-spending states receive below average resources—even counting federal funds. William L. Taylor and Dianne M. Piché put it this way: "[Our school finance system] operates to rob children born into poverty and locked into property-poor urban and rural areas of the basic resources that they need to achieve in public schools."[6]

Effects of Funding Disparities

In real education terms, do these expenditure disparities really make a difference in the services provided to schoolchildren? Jonathan Kozol (1992) provided a picture of just how important money is in individual

---

[6]See Volume II of this study.

schools. He compared the school facilities and programs available in the wealthy Chicago suburban New Trier Township High School with the threadbare educational offerings of the inner-city Du Sable and Goudy schools.

New Trier High School students can take advantage of superior science laboratories, up-to-date technology, and music and art facilities. Latin and six other foreign languages are offered. Electives include the literature of Nobel prize winners, aeronautics, criminal justice, and computer languages. The average class size is 24 children; special education classes hold 15. Each student has access to a personal counselor who works with only two dozen students. At Du Sable and Goudy, by contrast, laboratories are makeshift or nonexistent, there are no music or art classes and no playground. Compensatory education classes hold up to 40 students, and guidance counselors struggle with student loads of 420.

Kozol also described conditions at the Martin Luther King Junior High School in East St. Louis, Illinois. In 1989, while the school was being evacuated after a sewage backup in its kitchen, the school board announced budget cuts laying off 280 teachers, 25 teacher's aides, 166 cafeteria workers and cooks, and more than 30 maintenance workers. At East St. Louis High School, the 50-year old science laboratories are so outdated that they barely serve their purpose: Physics lab stations have holes where gas lines once fed Bunsen burners; the biology laboratory lacks lab tables, dissecting kits, and microscopes; a properly equipped chemistry laboratory cannot be used safely because the chemistry teacher has no lab assistants.

Students are at risk not only from poverty, but from the schools they attend.

Linda Darling-Hammond, Professor

Describing inner-city school conditions elsewhere, Kozol (1992, p. 5) wrote:

> In Boston, the press referred to . . ."death zones"—a specific reference to the rate of infant death in ghetto neighborhoods—but the feeling of the "death zone" often seemed to permeate the schools themselves. Looking around some of these inner-city schools, where filth and disrepair were worse than anything I'd seen in 1964, I often wondered why we would agree to let our children go to school in places where no politician, school board president, or business CEO would dream of working.

Kozol's images of schools with such serious funding shortfalls that they can barely provide minimal educational services are confirmed by a 1991 House of Representatives study (Taylor and Piché, 1991). According to that study, low-income districts were less likely to offer preschool child-development programs, more likely to stuff additional children into individual classrooms, sorely deficient in counseling and social services, and less likely to have as many teachers with advanced degrees or to offer as full a curriculum.

With the reduction of state and local resources, how can we best use Chapter 1 staff?

E. Ray Holt, School Superintendent

Based on the evidence, the Chapter 1 program as now designed and funded clearly cannot respond to the growing educational crisis in low-income areas. Chapter 1 funds are so broadly distributed nationwide that most districts, even with this extra money, cannot concentrate sufficient funds to make a significant difference in the quality of education provided to low-income students. Moreover, because of the large disparities in education resources between low-income and affluent school districts, the education of many Chapter 1 participants is less well funded, federal aid notwithstanding, than the education of other students in their own state or around the nation.

In a society committed to fairness, these findings point to the failure of a fundamental national value: the belief that all children deserve an equal chance in life. What message does it send to the child who leaves the poverty of his or her family and neighborhood to seek refuge for the day in what turns out to be the poverty of a school? Again quoting Kozol (1992, p. 154), who is questioning a student:

> "If the governor announced that he was going to combine you with the kids from Cherry Hill—everybody goes to one school maybe for the ninth grade and the tenth grade, everybody to the other school for both their final years—what would you say?" "As soon as it was announced they'd start remodeling," Luis replies. "You'd see progress very fast. Parents of white children, with their money, they'd come in and say, 'we need this fixed. Our kids deserve it.' So they'd back us up, you see, and there'd be changes."

3. CHAPTER 1 SERVICES AND STUDENT ACHIEVEMENT

Regardless of the inadequate funding of Chapter 1 and disparities in in- tra- and interstate finance, the fact remains that each school year feder- ally funded compensatory services are provided to some 5 million stu- dents in the nation's schools. Chapter 1 is clearly an important program. It focuses attention on the needs of disadvantaged students and provides services that would not otherwise be available in many schools.

Chapter 1 serves students who are typically in the bottom quarter of tested achievement. In many states, the *average* achievement level of these students is in the 15th to 20th percentile range, and many are in the bottom 10th percentile. More than half the students served are not poor, although many come from families with relatively low incomes. We dis- cuss below (1) the kinds of educational services provided to these youngsters and (2) the likelihood that these services will appreciably af- fect the quality of education in low-income communities.

Services

At the local level Chapter 1 is not a program at all, but a source of fund- ing that local districts and schools can use for virtually anything that ap- pears educationally reasonable. The variety of local program emphases reflects the flexibility built into the legislation. In Detroit, for example, individual school principals decide how their Chapter 1 funds will be spent. In the words of a Detroit school administrator, "There are as many delivery methods as there are teachers" (Miller, 1991). Some schools use instructional aides; some pull students out of regular classes to provide supplemental instruction; others provide instruction in the regular classroom.

Apart from different delivery systems, different schools deliver distinctly different services. The principal of Detroit's Herman Elementary School believes that everyone is entitled to a chance to learn in regular class- rooms from kindergarten through grade 2. But from grades 3 to 5, this school delivers extra assistance in the form of special laboratories and in-class tutoring through Chapter 1, which also pays for computer equip- ment, parent workshops, field trips, and mathematics and science teach- ers. Hanstein Elementary School, by contrast, focuses its Chapter 1 program on grades 1 and 2. Chapter 1 also supports equipment, supplies, and rewards for Hanstein children who read the most books (Miller, 1991).

A third Detroit school, White Elementary, serves children in all grades "strictly in rank order as to who needs it most," according to the princi- pal. Chapter 1 also supports an attendance program, a computer lab

Chapter 1 works and it increases the achievement of low- achieving, disad- vantaged students.

Hilda S. Pierce, Chapter 1 Reading Teacher

At any one time, half the United States is moving from in-class mod- els to pullouts, and the other half is moving from pull- outs to in-class.

Stanley Pogrow, Professor

(with equipment that children can take home), and bilingual education programs (Miller, 1991).

Schools in St. Charles Parish, Louisiana, have none of the flexibility of their Detroit counterparts. In St. Charles Parish, the district Chapter 1 coordinator decides where to concentrate funds, based on test scores and other compensatory services available to particular children. In 1991, the district provided reading in grades 1 through 5, but mathematics only in grades 3 through 5. The district coordinator believes that "reading is more important in the early grades" (Miller, 1991).

The best possible use of any funding increase would be to expand programs at the earliest level of education.

Marilyn McKnight, Teacher

None of the program decisions described above is educationally unsound. The educational offerings supported by Chapter 1 in Detroit and St. Charles Parish are among the most frequently cited services provided in compensatory education. Typically, funds are used for remedial reading and mathematics programs. Computer-assisted instruction, language arts, and English as a second language are also supported with Chapter 1 funds. In fact, Chapter 1 permits all of these programs and many others, including early childhood activities, extended-day kindergarten, health and nutrition services, integrated family services, counseling and social services, summer activities, dropout prevention efforts, and vocational and college counseling.

Unless children are made to see literacy as valuable and enjoyable, they will choose not to read and write.

Janet Tinari, Chapter 1 Chairperson, Education Association

The intensity of the services provided by Chapter 1 also fluctuates significantly. Clearly, it makes a difference whether a child receives one 30-minute period of reading or mathematics instruction a week, or five. Districts and schools, however, are caught on the horns of a dilemma: With limited funds, they are often forced to choose between providing intense remedial services to a limited number of children (generally those in the most severe need), or serving all eligible children by limiting the extra instruction each receives.

Measuring the intensity of services by the average caseload of Chapter 1 staff in 17 school districts, an Educational Testing Service study (Goertz et al., 1987) concluded that four districts spread services across their Chapter 1 populations and 13 concentrated resources. Case loads for Chapter 1 staff in the 17 school districts ranged from 28 to 100 students per staff member. The relative poverty of the districts (i.e., the number or concentration of low-income students) had no bearing on whether or not districts concentrated or spread resources. Poor districts were just as likely to spread or concentrate services as high-income districts.

Student Achievement

Against this backdrop, comes a large array of expensive national studies tracking the history of the program. Among the major reports finding their way into the policy debate throughout the life of Chapter 1:

- A 1969 report indicted local programs for such abuses as frivolous expenditures, serving ineligible schools, and poorly planned and executed programs (McClure and Martin, 1969).

- Reports from the National Institute of Education in 1976 and 1977 indicated that in specially selected, stable compensatory classrooms, participating first graders demonstrated reading gains of 12 months for each 7 months of instruction, and mathematics gains of 11 months. Third graders gained 8 months in reading and 12 months in mathematics (NIE, September 30, 1977).

- A massive study, begun during the presidency of Richard Nixon and completed during the tenure of Ronald Reagan, reported that compensatory services appear to have a positive effect in mathematics in grades 1 through 6, but in reading the effect is positive only in the first three grades (Carter, 1983).

- An interim 1992 report from an ongoing national assessment summarized research through 1988 as follows: Chapter 1 appeared to improve basic skills, did not teach higher-order skills, and was not integrated with regular school programs. Improvements in basic skills were not sustained over time (U.S. Department of Education, 1992).

In the context of Chapter 1's inadequate funding and rather limited services, it is not surprising that the program, on average, achieves modest short-term benefits. Moreover, given the diversity in service, these nationwide efforts at evaluation disguise the reality that many individual Chapter 1 programs achieve outstanding results. However, when the results of strong programs are added to those that are modest or weak, and when the tests used to measure progress often bear little relationship to the Chapter 1 program that was implemented in a particular school, the aggregate evaluation results provide little meaningful information.

Chapter 1 in the Context of the Regular School Program

Most evaluations have assessed Chapter 1 in isolation, without regard to the rest of the school program or to the curriculum of non-Chapter 1 students. Although the *Sustaining Effects* report (Carter, 1983) is now a decade old, it still represents the most exhaustive examination of what Chapter 1 looks like in the nation's schools. It is an almost unique evaluation in that it (1) examined services received by compensatory students in the context of services generally available in the school and (2) described the degree to which Chapter 1 actually delivers supplemental services in individual schools. Carter found the following:

- In the first and second grades, Chapter 1 and non-Chapter 1 students in the same school received essentially the same amount of reading instruction.

- From grades 3 to 6, Chapter 1 students received more reading instruction than their non-Chapter 1 peers (about 36 extra minutes a week in grade 3, and between 96 to 100 extra minutes each week in grades 4 through 6).

- From grades 1 through 6, Chapter 1 students received an average of about one additional hour a week of mathematics instruction.

- While in compensatory reading and mathematics activities, Chapter 1 students miss regular curriculum activities, most frequently, reading, mathematics, and other curriculum areas, in addition to gym, library visits, and study halls.

- Thus, Chapter 1 students have a gross gain in reading and mathematics instruction, but it is questionable whether the total instructional time is greater when the whole curriculum is considered.

Being pulled out of regular class gave students the feeling they were always playing catch-up.

Eugene D. Owens,
District Chapter 1
Coordinator

Some important implications flow from these conclusions. Assume, for the sake of argument, that each Chapter 1 student receives an average of two hours of additional instruction each week (divided between reading and mathematics) in the course of an elementary school year. Some will receive more; some, less; some will not receive instruction in both reading and mathematics. But two hours a week is not an unreasonable estimate for the sake of illustration. There are about 36 weeks in a 180-day school year. Each of these students, therefore, will receive about 72 hours of special instruction divided between reading and mathematics.

A 6-hour school day in a 180-day school year provides 1080 hours of available instruction time, of which the 72 hours of special instruction represents 6.7 percent. Concede that the instruction is sometimes of higher quality and more intense because it is more focused and delivered to smaller groups. Even so, expecting a program to produce unambiguous increases in achievement when the program accounts for only 6.7 percent of the student's annual instructional time is asking a lot.

The quality of the intervention will be only as effective as the quality of the personnel involved.

Linda F. Winfield,
Professor

How much extra progress can be expected from an average of 12 extra minutes a day each in reading and mathematics? Indeed, when most of the additional time is stolen from the rest of the curriculum, primarily in reading and mathematics, and when the instruction is delivered by aides rather than by trained teachers in some schools, the expectation of notable academic progress appears unrealistic.

In light of what compensatory services actually look like in the school—i.e., little additional instruction per day—the limited treatment currently provided by Chapter 1 seems highly unlikely to lead to major improvements in overall academic performance, although it can strengthen basic skills. Significant academic gains require a much more serious effort.

Chapter 1 in the Context of Other Categorical Programs

Chapter 1 is simply one among many federal, state, and local programs operating together to meet special needs in the schools, although it is by far the largest in terms of federal dollars. Each of these programs—for the disadvantaged, for those suffering disabilities, and for students with limited ability to speak English—has its own constituency and required audit trail, leading many observers to conclude that services at the local level are fragmented and that they depend less on student needs and more on keeping the books and intended beneficiaries straight.

While there is little disagreement about the potential benefits of improving the coordination among federal, state, and local programs and, indeed, of decreasing the proliferation of separate programs that have insufficient funding to make a difference, it would be futile to recommend combining the major federal categorical programs nationwide without fundamentally changing the way these programs are considered legislatively.

Unless the programs are considered as a unit, they will continue to have widely varying regulations, funding levels, and target groups. For example, while such programs as bilingual education and vocational education serve large numbers of low-income children, the programs are clearly not designed specifically for the low-income population group. The program for children with disabilities, to an even greater extent, cuts across all income levels.

Moreover, the federal program for children with disabilities provides only a small proportion of the funds needed to deliver the services required under the legislation. These requirements place a financial burden on school districts; some understandably respond by assigning children who can be labeled as either "special education" or "Chapter 1" students to Chapter 1 programs because the Chapter 1 programs are fully funded by the federal government.

Many of the commentaries that we received described potential benefits of combining funds from various programs. As one respondent, Christopher T. Cross, put it, "We need to step back from the profusion of federal programs aimed at helping poor and/or underachieving children (Title I, bilingual education, special education, etc.) and realize that children do not come with labels."[1] Cross also pointed out the obstacles at the federal level to coordinating these programs:

> Since the mid-1960s we have been caught in a cycle of reauthorizing various major programs in a clockwork fashion that guarantees that Congress and the executive never examine all of the programs serving K through 12 at one time. . . . Over time, the result has been that Congress has created separate subcommittees with jealously guarded jurisdictional lines that ensure that one set of lawmakers is unable to move be-

The biggest problem . . . relative to coordination is special education. . . . There is a desperate need to fund special education mandates adequately.

Albert Shanker,
President, National
Education
Association

Please do not combine or coordinate Chapter 1 with other programs. The only thing that would result would be less money for the children and more paperwork for the Chapter 1 teacher.

Connie Hay,
Chapter 1 Reading
Specialist

---

[1]See Volume II of this report.

yond those narrow confines. Similarly, the federal executive branch, state education agencies, local school districts, and even individual schools have come to reflect those divisions. . . . It is not surprising that states and local districts have almost identical structures. Each is charged with seeing to the partial needs of a child. Not one single office is charged with integrating programs or with seeing that the total needs of children are met.

In short, while coordination of services to the child at the local level remains a highly desirable goal and many schools find ways to make it work, it is unrealistic to recommend commingling the programs on a national basis in the absence of a consistent framework for education legislation at the federal level.

Chapter 1's Multiple Purposes

Let's determine all the services affecting a single child and build a coordinated approach to meeting children's and family's needs.

Edward P. Keller, Deputy Director, Education Association

The Title I/Chapter 1 legislation is based on a "recognition of the special educational needs of children of low-income families and the impact of concentrations of low-income families on the ability of local educational agencies to provide educational programs which meet such needs." The statute recognizes the special educational needs of other groups, including children of migrant parents, Native American children, and handicapped, neglected, and delinquent children.

With regard to children from low-income families, the legislative intent appears to be sharply focused: All low-income children, whatever their individual strengths or weaknesses, have special educational needs that many school districts do not address. Further, the impact of large concentrations of low-income families means that school districts have trouble meeting these special needs. At a certain point, the *concentration* of low-income students requires far more expenditures than simply an arithmetic multiplier based on the number of poor children.

The next section of the statute, however, appears to shift direction: Congress declares it to be the policy of the United States to provide assistance to state and local educational agencies "to meet the special needs of such *educationally deprived children* at the preschool, elementary, and secondary levels."

Chapter 1 programming should emphasize the integration of Chapter 1 services into an enhanced regular curriclum.

Keith Geiger, President, National Education Association

The later wording shifted the focus of the legislation from the educational needs of low-income children to the needs of educationally deprived children. In practice, this change has meant that while the funding formula drives funds to the district and then normally to the school, based on counts of *low-income* youngsters, only youngsters deemed *educationally deprived* on the basis of achievement measures are eligible for Chapter 1 services. This restriction, in turn, creates discrete "special" services for a relatively small proportion of the student body, even in low-income districts.

As a practical matter, the program may not have enjoyed other alternatives. Given the shortcomings in funding available for Chapter 1 relative to the needs of low-income school districts, the focus on low-achieving students functioned as a rationing device when only a small proportion of students in each school could be served.

Because funds are spread so broadly across states, districts, and schools, the neediest schools rarely have the resources required to do much more than provide remedial basic skills programs. The funds certainly are not adequate to improve the quality of education generally—for poor children or for low-achieving children. For understandable reasons (primarily financial), as the program has developed, it has come to be understood as supplemental services for, and only for, the lowest-achieving children in communities throughout the nation.

For the sake of convenience, this report has referred to Chapter 1 students as "low-income." But, in fact, most of the students receiving services are not poor, according to the official definition of poverty. According to the *Sustaining Effects* study (Carter, 1983), an estimated 1.23 million low-income, elementary-school children and nearly 1.7 million nonpoor children received Chapter 1 services in 1983. At the same time, nearly 2.2 million low-income children did not receive compensatory services although they attended schools offering Chapter 1 or other compensatory programs. While six out of ten Chapter 1 participants came from the bottom two-fifths of family income, four out of ten came from the top three-fifths, including 8 percent from the highest fifth.

What is needed in this plethora of education bashing is to explore new alternatives and to provide better educational opportunities for low-income students.

John V. Corcoran, District Chapter 1 Director

The point is that the program's multiple purposes—an amalgamation aimed at assisting low-income districts while also providing funds for low-achieving children in wealthy districts—have produced a difficult combination of objectives. These objectives encompass raising the achievement of the lowest-performing students in a large proportion of the nation's schools, while at the same time improving the overall quality of education in low-income communities—all without sufficient resources. While it would not be feasible to limit Chapter 1 services only to low-income students, Chapter 1 can be reframed to increase significantly the resources available to the nation's poorest districts and schools.[2]

The findings presented in this section are the foundation for the main arguments of the report:

- Although the objective of Chapter 1 was sound from the start, the program was never implemented with the resources required to make it succeed.

---

[2]Chapter 1 services cannot be limited to low-income students because (1) in schools that select children for special services, it does not make sense educationally to select these children based on poverty criteria rather than on their educational needs and (2) even in the poorest schools, schoolwide projects would reach some children who were not technically poor, although many of these children would come from families that were close to the poverty line.

- Policymakers and educators have ignored the obvious in their evaluations: Chapter 1 cannot be better than the schools that it seeks to help.

- The issue is not whether Chapter 1 works, but whether the schools serving Chapter 1 students are adequate.

The basic approach to Chapter 1 should now be rethought. Strategies that were appropriate in 1965, or even in 1988, the last time Chapter 1 was amended, will not suit the new demands of the next decade. The pressures on schools have accelerated dramatically in recent years. These pressures are likely to worsen as more low-income children arrive at the schoolhouse door. Indeed, because of the way the world is changing, today's inadequate strategies are even less likely to pass muster ten years hence, in 2003.

4. IMPROVING THE EDUCATION OF LOW-INCOME CHILDREN

What can the United States do to place low-income children on a more equal footing with their more advantaged peers? How could such an effort be structured? How much would it cost? A major theme of the commentaries that we received was the need for significant increases in the concentration of Chapter 1 funds to address the severe educational problems in schools with high proportions of low-income children and the serious underfunding of these schools.[1] Because of the high correlation between poverty and educational problems, children in poor schools need substantially more educational resources, yet they receive a lot less.

Many children continue not to be served because funds are limited.

John A. Pfaff,
Principal/Chapter 1
Coordinator

This section recommends a three-part federal strategy for meeting the needs of low-income students:

- Increase Chapter 1 funding for the nation's lowest-income school districts and schools.

- Reformulate Chapter 1 to encourage fundamental improvements in the quality of education available to low-income children of all achievement levels.

- Use a separate general aid program to provide incentives for equalizing overall funding within states.

Increase Funding for the Lowest-Income School Districts and Schools

The concentration of funding requires giving far more weight to poverty than is now given in directing Chapter 1 funds to districts and schools. Under the formula that we propose, almost all of the districts currently eligible for Chapter 1 would continue to receive some funding. In practice, the level of funding in a district would depend on the combined effects of (1) the overall Chapter 1 appropriations and (2) the degree of weighting for low-income districts built into the formula. Because of the needs of low-income school districts, consideration should be given to the use of a formula weighted by concentration of poor children regardless of the overall level of Chapter 1 appropriations.[2]

---

[1]See Volume II of this report.

[2]Parts of the discussion in this section of proposed changes in the Chapter 1 funding formula and of the use of a separate aid program to provide incentives to equalize funding are drawn from Volume III of this report.

Another approach to increasing the concentration of funds would allocate Chapter 1 resources only to districts with high concentrations of poverty. Clearly, there is a strong argument for this option, given the large inequalities in school finance and the special needs of schools with high concentrations of poor children. Technically, the option is relatively straightforward and would make it possible to serve larger numbers of low-income children with more diverse programs than is now the case.

An arbitrary demarcation line of this type, however, would force policymakers to choose between (1) setting the poverty cutoff so low that the objective would be defeated or (2) eliminating Chapter 1 funding in a large number of school districts (many with significant numbers of low-income children), thereby causing significant disruption of services to thousands of schools and millions of children. The option of funding only the lowest-income districts would be easier to introduce if the Chapter 1 program were not yet in operation.

The existing funding mechanism distributes funds mainly according to the number of low-income children in each county or school district, but it spreads the available funds thinly and widely.[3] The formula takes little account of the disproportionate educational problems faced by districts with high concentrations of poor children in their schools and the widespread underfunding of these schools.

The changes proposed in this section would alter the distribution pattern by providing substantially greater aid *per low-income child* to the districts and schools with the most severe poverty-related problems. The proposed changes include the following three key elements:

- Merging the present Basic Grant and Concentration Grant formulas into a single formula that allocates more Chapter 1 aid per low-income child to districts where the percentage of low-income children is higher.

- Distributing funds first to states and then to the school districts in each state.

- Requiring each school district to distribute Chapter 1 resources so as to strongly favor schools with high concentrations of low-income pupils.

It would not be feasible for the federal government to allocate funds directly to these schools for two reasons: First, the lack of a national body of data on numbers of poor children in individual schools effectively precludes direct allocation. Second, even if direct distribution to schools were technically feasible, it might create undesirable incentives for the school district.

---

[3]See Section 2, above, "Delivering Federal Funds."

Because the distribution of poor children among schools often depends on deliberate district choices—e.g., with respect to pupil assignment, busing, and the operation of magnet schools—a system of direct allocation on the basis of school-level poverty might encourage districts to segregate their low-income pupils in particular schools. For both reasons, we must take the indirect route of first channeling funds to high-poverty districts and then delegating the school-level distribution to district authorities.

Use a Consolidated, Weighted Formula

Currently, 90 percent of Chapter 1 funds are allocated according to a Basic Grant formula that does not take poverty concentration into account; the remaining 10 percent are allocated according to a Concentration Grant formula that has little concentrating effect. In place of this two-part formula, we recommend a single, consolidated formula that gives extra weight to low-income children in places with high percentages of poverty.

Put more emphasis on concentration formulas that would restrict the use of Chapter 1 funds to schools with high concentrations of poor students.

Jere Brophy, Professor

Although this type of weighted formula could be used to distribute Chapter 1 funds to counties, the units that receive allocations under the present formula, we recommend, for reasons explained below, that Chapter 1 funds be distributed first to states and then to the school districts in each state. The weighted formula could be applied at both the state and district levels, or only at the district level.[4] The discussion below focuses on district-level allocations.

The specific degree of extra weighting may be debated, but for illustrative purposes a simplified example of increasing weights for school districts with increasing ranges of poverty concentration follows:

Percentage of Low-Income Children in District	Weight per Low-Income Child
Up to 20	1.00
21 to 40	1.25
41 to 60	1.60
Over 60	2.00

Under such a formula, each district would receive aid based on a weighted count of its poor children. Therefore, districts with substantial proportions of low-income children would receive significantly more aid

---

[4]At the state level, the current proxy for cost of education—state per pupil expenditures—might also be replaced with a more accurate indicator of educational costs. See Volume III of this report.

for each low-income child. For example, using the illustrative weights shown above, an urban or rural district with, say, 70 percent of its children from families with income below the poverty line would receive twice as much Chapter 1 money *for each low-income child* as an upper-income suburban district with, say, only 8 percent of its children from poor families.

A more refined version of the weighted formula would calculate each district's weighting factor according to a continuous sliding scale. This would avoid the inequities that could arise using a set of discrete weights like those illustrated (for example, a district with, say, 59.5 percent poor children, falling just short of qualifying for the maximum allocation per low-income child).[5]

Distribute Funds to States, Then to School Districts

Under the present formula, Chapter 1 funds are allocated to counties on the basis of county-level poverty counts. There are no state allocations per se. Each state is responsible for allocating funds to the school districts in each county according to the number of poor children in each district, using a state-selected measure of poverty. This county-level formula was adopted originally for the practical reason that national data on child poverty from the decennial census were available for counties but not for school districts.

Some districts with high concentrations of poverty are not located in counties with high poverty and do not receive concentration funds.

Robert Leininger, State Superintendent of Education

The retention of the county-level formula, however, would reduce the accuracy of allocating Chapter 1 funds in relation to poverty concentration when counties contain districts with very different concentrations. Los Angeles county, for example, includes extremely wealthy districts like Beverly Hills and very poor, almost all-minority districts like Compton. If Los Angeles County were to receive an allocation of Chapter 1 funds based on its countywide average poverty rate, and if those funds were then distributed to districts according to anything like the present subcounty allocation rules, the poorest districts would not receive aid commensurate with their high poverty concentrations. Poor districts would fare better if California's Chapter 1 funds were distributed to individual districts across the state, without regard to county, using the type of weighted funds-allocation formula suggested above. We recommend, therefore, that serious consideration be given to switching from the current formula to a two-tier structure in which Chapter 1

---

[5]The same formula could also incorporate the principle that scarce Chapter 1 funds should not be allocated to districts with only minimal poverty-related problems in their schools. For example, considering that the national child-poverty percentage is now almost 20 percent, the formula might be designed to allocate zero aid to districts that have fewer than, say, 8 to10 percent low-income children. Establishing such a threshold would reduce the amount of additional Chapter 1 funding necessary to provide significant extra aid to places with high poverty concentrations.

funds would be distributed first to the states and then to the school districts in each state.

Two possibilities exist for measuring poverty for the purpose of allocating Chapter 1 funds directly to the school districts in each state. First, the Census Bureau's current effort to map 1990 census data onto school district boundaries may yield valid district-level poverty data. Such data would enable Congress to write a formula that specifies completely how funds should be allocated, based on poverty counts, down to the district level.

Second, each state could be given limited discretion to select a state-specific poverty measure to be used in allocating funds among its districts. Based on experience with the subcounty allocation process, most states would probably select an indicator based either on eligibility for free school lunches or on numbers of recipients of Aid to Families with Dependent Children (AFDC) benefits.

The federal government would have to exercise close oversight over each state's choices of factors and, of course, would specify the procedure for weighting the counts of poor children to reflect each district's poverty concentration. Given these two options, problems of data availability would not appear to preclude the shift to a two-tier formula.

Favor the High-Poverty Schools in Each District

School districts also should give priority to their highest-poverty schools in allocating Chapter 1 resources. The objective is to increase substantially the resource levels available to these schools so that they can fundamentally change their education program. Districts could allocate funds to schools using a weighted formula comparable to that proposed for district allocations, giving extra weight to schools with high proportions of low-income children. This formula could be combined with the principle that Chapter 1 funds should be allocated only to schools above a specified poverty threshold, for example, 10 percent.

We further recommend that school districts use only poverty criteria, rather than the current mix of poverty and achievement criteria, to allocate funds to schools. The use of poverty criteria would eliminate current perverse incentives that increase funds for schools as the number of low-achieving children increases, while decreasing funds for schools reporting achievement gains.

Finally, the proposed strategy should be implemented so as to ensure that the federal funds do not replace what otherwise would have been spent. A strategy designed to provide sufficient resources to high-poverty schools becomes meaningless if those resources simply replace state and local expenditures.

The absence of census data updates allows funds to be distributed based on data that may be up to 12 years old.

Bill Honig, State Superintendent

Poor performance is not the only indicator of deprivation or need.

Chris Pipho, State Relations Director, Education Association

Large intradistrict resource inequities among schools exist despite the requirement that the level of service in Chapter 1 schools be at least comparable to that in non-Chapter 1 schools before the addition of compensatory funds. For example, data gathered in connection with the *Rodriguez v. Anton* school finance litigation in Los Angeles showed that the per pupil expenditures in some schools were almost twice as high as those in others.[6] Moreover, while per pupil expenditures varied widely even for schools with similar population characteristics, schools with higher than average proportions of Hispanic students (defined as 15 percent above the district average) received, on average, significantly lower levels of resources.

Why [school districts] would hire the least qualified personnel for children with the greatest needs defies logic.

Virginia R. L. Plunkett, State Chapter 1 Coordinator

Differences in teachers' experience and education which, in turn, determine their salaries, accounted for a large part of the gap. More often than not, the "best" teachers, including experienced teachers offered greater choice in school assignments because of their seniority, avoid high-poverty schools. As a result, low-income and minority students have less contact with the best-qualified and more experienced teachers, the teachers most likely to master the kinds of instructional strategies considered effective for all students (Oakes, 1990).

We recommend, therefore, strengthening the comparability regulation so that it creates real resource equality among schools before the addition of Chapter 1 funds. Such a requirement would increase substantially the total resources available to the lowest-income schools. The current variation in dollar value of the assets in schools can vary by a factor of two. A large part of the difference is caused by teacher allocation: The neediest schools usually get the teachers with the lowest levels of experience and education. While we are not recommending a specific approach, Chapter 1 could promote real comparability, for example, by requiring that the dollar per pupil operating costs of schools must be equal (say, within 5 percent) before Chapter 1 funds are made available.

Reformulate Chapter 1 to Encourage Better Education for Low-Income Children of All Achievement Levels

Provided they are sufficient for the purpose, Chapter 1 funds directed to low-income communities should be used to encourage schoolwide improvement in the designated schools. This recommendation is based on the evidence that low-, moderate-, and high-achieving children in schools with large concentrations of poor children have fewer educational opportunities than do children in more affluent schools.

---

[6]We are indebted to Stephen P. Klein of RAND for this example.

Robert Slavin, a Johns Hopkins University researcher, puts it this way:

> [Research finds that] regardless of their own personal characteristics, poor students in schools with large numbers of poor children achieve less than equally poor students in less disadvantaged schools. Students in schools serving disadvantaged students deserve assistance even if they are not low achievers themselves. We should be particularly concerned about poor and minority students who may be doing well enough to avoid Chapter 1 identification but are still not achieving their full potential. . . . [Yet] the poorest school in a wealthy district may receive significant Chapter 1 funds, while a far poorer school in a large urban district will not, because the urban school is not as poor as others in the district.[7]

By reorienting Chapter 1 to serve all low-income children and by directing resources to meet that objective, Chapter 1 would have the potential to go beyond remedial basic skills instruction to provide significant improvements in the education available to low-income students, whatever their level of tested achievement.

Funding for Schoolwide Projects

Relatively few Chapter 1 schools nationwide currently have adequate resources to make fundamental improvements in their education programs. Under the Chapter 1 funds allocation changes recommended above, programmatic possibilities for the poorest Chapter 1 schools could change dramatically. Many more schools would have the resources needed to make comprehensive changes in their educational offerings, i.e., to encourage more schoolwide projects with more money behind them.

Under existing law, schools with an enrollment of 75 percent or more poor students are permitted to use Chapter 1 resources to make overall improvements in their education programs (schoolwide projects) rather than limiting services to selected students. Some 2000 schools have implemented schoolwide projects to date, although more than 9000 schools are eligible. Many of these schools currently do not have the level of resources required to make schoolwide projects a viable option.

The level of Chapter 1 funding needed to make the widespread use of schoolwide projects a realistic option in the poorest communities will clearly depend on many factors. These include a school's per pupil expenditure, local costs of education, the characteristics of the existing educational program, start-up and training costs, and the special needs of the students served. While it would be unwise to set specific national funding levels for individual schoolwide projects, a general estimate of the

Chapter 1 should be designed to encourage continuously rising levels of achievement.

Lauren B. Resnick, Professor

Lower the eligibility threshold [for schoolwide projects] from 75% poverty to 50%.

Joseph A. Fernandez, Superintendent of Schools

---

[7]See Volume II of this report.

number of schoolwide projects that could be supported at various Chapter 1 appropriations levels is needed.

The focus on elementary skills is unlikely to lead to jobs that will maintain a decent standard of living.

Charles S. Benson, Director of Research Organization

A review of additional costs of schoolwide projects, magnet schools, and other "innovative programs" shows wide variations in per pupil expenditures. In Philadelphia, for example, schoolwide projects received an average of approximately $720 per *enrolled* student (i.e., including every student attending the school, not only Chapter 1-eligible students) in the 1992–1993 school year; the range was between $500 and $1000 per student.[8] Similar variability holds for magnet schools. Additional costs of magnet schools in one district ranged from $400 to $1300 per pupil (Blank, 1989). Another district added between .5 and 5 additional staff members in magnet elementary schools, while a magnet high school received 9.5 additional staff to serve 325 students.[9]

Robert Slavin's *Success for All* program spends about $1000 extra per pupil, while the figure for the *Reading Recovery* program is slightly higher. Sweden is reported to spend two to three times the national average on schools with high proportions of disadvantaged children (Clune, 1992).

I received only about $30 worth of paperback books this year. Everything else I needed was purchased with my own checkbook.

Barbara Funderburk, Teacher

The 1965 Title I legislation stated that local education agencies were eligible to receive grants equal to 40 percent of the average per pupil expenditure in the state (but not less than 80 percent nor more than 120 percent of national average expenditure per pupil), multiplied by the number of eligible poor children ages 5–17 (Compilation of Federal Education Laws, 1991). This figure is considerably higher than the current national average expenditure per Chapter 1 student, which is estimated at about $1100 (based on appropriations for the 1992–1993 school year).[10]

While these diverse examples of per pupil expenditures serve as a starting point for projecting Chapter 1 costs, they clearly cannot provide specific guidance. First, the expenditure figures vary greatly; second, systematic data are not available for each school on *overall* expenditures, on student needs, or on how the funds were used. Therefore, projections of Chapter 1 costs should not be based simply on what current programs spend but should also consider the broader context—school finance inequalities, as well as the greater educational needs of low-income children. In combination, these factors provide the foundation for making a rough estimate of the expenditure level required to make a difference.

---

[8]We are indebted to Katherine Conner of the Philadelphia Public Schools for these cost figures.

[9]We are indebted to Jeffrey R. Henig, The George Washington University, for these figures.

[10]The Chapter 1 per pupil expenditure typically cited is $800, based on FY1989 appropriations. The $1100 estimate used here reflects the increase in appropriations between FY1989 and FY1992, assuming that student participation remained constant.

Based on these broad considerations, we have selected a Chapter 1 expenditure per enrolled student (as defined above) equivalent to the nationwide average expenditure per Chapter 1 student of $1100. That amount represents a 20 percent increment in funding relative to the U.S. average per pupil expenditure of $5500.

The $1100 expenditure figure is intended to serve as a guideline for estimating the overall level of Chapter 1 funding required to provide a critical mass of resources to the nation's lowest-income schools. It is not intended as the basis for legislating specific funding levels for individual schools.

With a per pupil Chapter 1 expenditure of $1100, a school with an enrollment of 500 students would receive $550,000 in Chapter 1 funds. In many cases, however, the proposed revenue increments still would not raise per pupil expenditures to the level of those in affluent districts. The increase would nevertheless provide a realistic opportunity for participating schools to make comprehensive educational improvements.

Table 2 shows the estimated national cost of funding schoolwide projects at the per pupil expenditures proposed above in schools where the proportion of low-income students ranges from 75 percent to 60 percent.

Table 2

ESTIMATED COSTS OF FUNDING SCHOOLWIDE PROJECTS AT VARIOUS SCHOOL POVERTY LEVELS

School Poverty Level	Eligible Elementary Schools		
	%	No.	Estimated Cost
75%	21	7,908	$3,836,170,800
70%	26	9,561	$4,638,041,100
65%	31	11,475	$5,566,522,500
60%	38	14,359	$6,965,550,900

School Poverty Level	All Eligible Schools		
	%	No.	Estimated Cost
75%	20	9,301	$5,043,932,300
70%	24	11,303	$6,129,616,900
65%	29	13,515	$7,329,184,500
60%	35	16,744	$9,080,271,200

SOURCE: The percentage and number of eligible schools are taken from M. A. Millsap, M. Moss, and B. Gamse (February 1993). "Chapter 1 in Public Schools, Draft Final Report." Cambridge, Mass.: Abt Associates.

NOTE: The estimated costs for elementary schools assume $485,100 per schoolwide project, based on average enrollment of 441 students in U.S. public elementary schools, at $1100 per student (the estimated average expenditure per Chapter 1 student in 1992-1993). The estimated costs for all eligible schools assumes $542,300 per schoolwide project, based on average enrollment of 493 students in U.S. public elementary and secondary schools, at $1100 per student. These cost projections are rough approximations because the data required to make more precise estimates are not available. For example, school enrollment figures are based on average enrollments nationwide, rather than on average enrollments in high-poverty districts.

If the proposed level of funding were provided to the 9301 schools with poverty percentages of 75 percent or higher, the estimated cost would exceed $5 billion; if the 16,744 schools with poverty percentages of 60 percent or higher were served, the estimated cost would come to about $9 billion.

These estimates include only the costs of funding schoolwide projects; they do not include the costs of funding the remaining Chapter 1 schools at current levels. Table 3 displays the total estimated national costs. The costs, of course, would be lower if the formula weights were applied so as to reduce funding for the more affluent schools.

A funding level of approximately $9.1 billion would provide the critical mass of resources needed to make significant educational improvements to schools with an enrollment of 75 percent or more poor children, while continuing to fund the other schools at current levels. A funding level of $12.3 billion would serve schools with an enrollment of 60 percent or more poor children—that is, more than 16,000 schools or approximately one-third of the nation's Chapter 1 schools.

The Case for Schoolwide Projects

Many of the commentaries received as part of this study stressed the importance of using Chapter 1 funds to improve the school as a whole,

Table 3

ESTIMATED COSTS OF FUNDING SCHOOLWIDE AND CHAPTER 1
REGULAR PROJECTS

School Poverty Level	Elementary Schoolwide Projects[a]	Remaining Chapter 1 Funding[b]	Total
75%	$3,836,170,800	$4,170,144,000	$8,006,314,800
70%	$4,638,041,100	$3,995,587,200	$8,633,628,300
65%	$5,566,522,500	$3,793,468,800	$9,359,991,300
60%	$6,965,550,900	$3,488,918,400	$10,454,469,300

School Poverty Level	All Schoolwide Projects[a]	Remaining Chapter 1 Funding[b]	Total
75%	$5,043,932,300	$4,023,043,200	$9,066,975,500
70%	$6,129,616,900	$3,811,632,000	$9,941,248,900
65%	$7,329,184,500	$3,578,044,800	$10,907,229,300
60%	$9,080,271,200	$3,237,062,400	$12,317,333,600

[a]From Table 2, above.

[b]Based on 47,398 Chapter 1 schools minus the number of schoolwide projects x 96 (average number of Chapter 1 students per school) x $1100 (average expenditure per Chapter 1 student).

rather than focusing on supplemental services for individual students. While supplemental services have benefited many children, they may also create, in some settings, tracking and uncoordinated educational programs. Many analysts therefore favor the use of Chapter 1 funds for schoolwide reform, arguing that overall improvements in the quality of regular classroom instruction will meet the needs of all low-income children.

In extending Chapter 1, Congress and the administration have an excellent opportunity to rethink the assumptions that have guided the program since its enactment in 1965, particularly around the issue of schoolwide improvement. Early federal efforts to assist education rested on the assumption that schools were, for the most part, functioning fairly well but that disadvantaged students needed "something extra."

A corollary to this thinking was that schools generally neglected poor and minority children and that federal assistance could encourage a more equitable alignment of local school priorities. Together, these assumptions led logically to a program that targeted specific students for "extra" services and limited the additional services only to those eligible.

Many things have changed since these programs were formulated. Educators and policymakers have expressed concern that a program of additional services can often substitute for the instruction that children would receive in their school's regular instruction program. In some schools, the special instruction has not kept pace with the curriculum improvements instituted in the regular school program.

In addition, since the early 1980s, analysts have pointed out that federal programs compete with not only the regular instructional program but also with each other: Because other state and federal "categorical" programs patterned themselves after Chapter 1, many analysts have concluded that the cumulative effect of multiple special-service programs has damaged the schools' ability to deliver high-quality regular instruction (Hill et al., 1990).

Moreover, a combination of poverty, immigration, weak local economies, and program fragmentation have rendered many schools incapable of serving the majority of their students. With dropout rates exceeding 50 percent in some schools and a serious lack of resources, it is hard to argue either that students need "just a little extra," or that a small minority of students suffers from selective neglect.

Many of these students need help. Yet, Chapter 1 reaches relatively few of them, and only in narrow instructional areas. The case for using Chapter 1 funds for schoolwide improvement is, therefore, attractive on several grounds:

The overdose of remediation that now characterizes academic work supported by Chapter 1 fails to motivate students and tends to lower the expectations of their teachers.

Harold Howe II, Professor

Chapter 1 is often one more label applied to students who already have too many labels.

John A. Murphy, Superintendent of Schools

- Some schools have so many low-income students that there is little point in distinguishing among them.

- Some schools are so pervasively inadequate and underfunded that they need basic reform, not the addition of a few services on the margin.

- Some low-income schools have such distinctive needs that a centrally designed program of supplementary services cannot meet school-specific needs.

These factors apply particularly to many urban schools and to schools with large proportions of immigrant children, where ethnic backgrounds, languages, and prior academic preparation vary significantly.

Nature of Schoolwide Projects

But if the case for schoolwide projects in many schools is clear, the nature of these projects is less so. Although schoolwide efforts are frequently advocated, the term is rarely defined. It may mean:

- Continuing special supplementary services, but making them available to all students in a classroom or school.

- Providing specific instructional staff or equipment, but permitting schools (rather than the central Chapter 1 office) to decide how resources will be used.

- Giving schools real dollars that may be used to purchase resources needed to strengthen the instructional program for all students.

Chapter 1 staff are prevented by law from working with groups that include non-Chapter 1 students.

Linda Brown, State Supervisor of Compensatory Education

The first alternative responds to two criticisms of Chapter 1: (1) the argument that classmates of Chapter 1 students are rarely highly advantaged and should share in the benefits of supplementary services and (2) the conclusion that managing distinct programs for particular subsets of students weakens the basic school program. But this first option is still a supplemental service, a marginal approach that does not support general improvements in schools' basic services.

Although the second alternative maintains a distinct identity for Chapter 1 resources, it also makes these resources a general school asset. It both responds to the criticism that Chapter 1 stands apart from the school's regular program and offers the possibility that Chapter 1 can encourage a more fundamental reform across the entire school. Schools are permitted to obtain only those additional resources—for example, specialized staff or equipment—that Chapter 1 provides. But because the services may be more like those the school already provides, all students are likely to receive some benefit—for example, slightly smaller class sizes or more time with specialized teachers or equipment—and the overall school program will not change much, if at all.

The third alternative, by providing fungible resources that may be used for almost any educational purpose, depending on boundaries set by law, changes the character of what Chapter 1 puts into the school. "Any educational purpose" could include:

- Hiring additional teachers or aides
- Covering additional time for current school staff for planning purposes, after-school or weekend tutoring, or training
- Hiring consultants or instructional specialists
- Providing bonuses for teachers with scarce skills, or incentive pay to encourage teachers to staff schools they had previously avoided
- Purchasing books and equipment, or comprehensive reform assistance.

Chapter 1 will never realize its full potential until the program provides quality training and is staffed with the best teachers.

Donald L. Carter, State Chapter 1 Consultant

Management of Schoolwide Projects

In the first two alternatives above, all students in a Chapter 1 school can have access to Chapter 1-funded resources. In the third alternative, the identity of Chapter 1-funded resources is deliberately obscured in the hope they will be used toward general school improvement. Although all three make it difficult to audit the exact uses of federal funds and to measure the productivity of federal contributions, the first two are less controversial at the district and school levels. Neither of the first two eliminates the rationale for systemwide Chapter 1 offices or the need for centrally identified and paid groups of Chapter 1 teachers or aides.

Managerially, the third—most controversial—alternative requires the most radical change. Because it proposes to eliminate the "project" conception of Chapter 1, the program would no longer be a set of readily identifiable activities, whether implemented and defined by central school district staff or developed by individual schools. Chapter 1 would no longer be a program coexisting with others in the same building and interacting with them only as staff members took the initiative. It would, instead, be a set of fungible resources intended to help review and revise everything that happens instructionally in the school.

[When] students are treated as whole persons, and not just as temporary occupants of one of 30 seats in a room, they feel cared for; they feel respected.

Maxine Skopov, Teacher

Some schools have been criticized for becoming holding companies for discrete activities funded from the outside, owned by individual staff members, and more responsive to funding sources than local needs. According to this critique, no one in these schools is responsible for the child's overall development or for developing a well-coordinated educational program.

Despite its difficulty, the third alternative is the only one of the three that would respond fully to this critique. It is the most powerful of the three, but its strength—the ability to break down fragmentation in the schools—cannot be fully implemented unless the other sources of fragmentation are also broken down. Decategorization of Chapter 1 will be more effective if other similar categories (e.g., special programs for bilingual education, vocational education, and so on) also are coordinated with the regular school program.

Potential Benefits and Cautions

Chapter 1 funds should be used to benefit all students, especially when most of the school population is poor and educationally disadvantaged.

Ronald S. Schneider, Chapter 1 Schoolwide Project Facilitator

Improved Education. Adequately funded, schoolwide projects provide an opportunity to make fundamental improvements in the quality of education available in low-income communities. They do so by increasing resources to the neediest schools, providing services to low-income children at all achievement levels, and facilitating the design of a range of educational programs.

With additional resources, policymakers can expect a substantial increase in the number of schools in low-income districts that can choose to implement some of today's more innovative education programs. Such programs include Sizer's *Coalition of Essential Schools*, Slavin's *Success For All*, Levin's *Accelerated Schools*, Comer's *Community Schools Model*, Pogrow's *HOTS (Higher Order Thinking Skills)* program, and Clay's *Reading Recovery* program. The many existing options for improving the education of low-income children can be realistically considered only if sufficient funds are available to implement them.

The emphasis [on targeting individual students] leads to programs that facilitate monitoring rather than maximizing student learning.

Gene Wilhoit, Director, Education Association

Options can be drawn from the diverse successful educational practices currently operating throughout the country. These practices include the reorganization of schools to encourage smaller school and class size, upgraded course offerings, "preventive" tutorial programs in reading, remedial basic skills programs, programs that focus on conceptual and problem-solving skills, accelerated science and mathematics programs, programs that incorporate technology to teach a wide range of subject matters and skills, and college and career counseling programs. These are the same opportunities routinely available in affluent neighborhoods.

Many schools may strike off in different directions, offering magnet school specialties in mathematics or science or other innovative educational programs. Some schools might apply part of the resources to train teachers in new educational practices or to obtain technical assistance—a first principle of effective educational innovation, as many of our respondents emphasized.

A school might reduce class size substantially, provide individual tutoring, build a state-of-the-art science laboratory, counsel students and families, coordinate health and social services, offer special programs for low-income students of all ability levels, or provide after-school services. Equally important, these schools would be more likely to attract high-quality teachers and principals because the educational possibilities and working environments would be enhanced.

Supplemental Instruction. The emphasis on schoolwide projects does not cancel the need for supplemental instruction or individual tutoring for particular students in some schools. Indeed, a blanket recommendation for schoolwide projects, universally applied, responds no better to the diversity of individual school and student needs than the prevailing, nearly universal practice of supplemental services for low-achieving students in designated schools. The new orientation simply provides options.

The categorical nature of Chapter 1 is a strength in itself.

Ted D. Kimbrough, Superintendent of Schools

Moreover, Chapter 1 resources should continue to focus on supplemental services in schools that do not receive sufficient funds to implement schoolwide projects. As some commentaries noted, if the current limited Chapter 1 resources went into overall school budgets, many children now receiving special services would probably lose them, while the quality of the educational program would not improve noticeably.

It is hardly meaningful to recommend schoolwide projects in a school that receives only enough Chapter 1 funds to support (as is often the case) one aide or a part-time teacher who has time to work only with children who score below the 15th or 20th percentile in reading. Educational choices are limited by funding—the question of the "optimum" Chapter 1 program (whether schoolwide projects or services to individually selected students are the best approach) cannot be separated from the level and allocation of resources.

With the in-class model, one teacher was so loud with her students that the small group I worked with couldn't hear me.

Anonymous Teacher

The argument is made, however, to continue to permit schools with high poverty concentrations (perhaps reducing the criterion from 75 percent to 65 or 70 percent) to implement schoolwide projects even if funding does not increase substantially. In this view, supplemental services cannot begin to address the widespread educational problems in high-poverty schools. Permitting schoolwide projects in these schools is a reasonable option.

If schoolwide projects are widely adopted, however, policymakers should be realistic about what the projects can—and cannot—accomplish. Permitting schoolwide projects is not the same as funding them adequately; without sufficient resources, schoolwide projects are unlikely to translate into significant schoolwide improvement.

Limitations of the Federal Role. The preceding analysis of alternative programs illustrates the approaches that might be used if more resources were available for low-income schools. In our view, however, the federal government should not prescribe programmatic matters. According to evidence from numerous sources, the federal government cannot intervene productively in local decisions about education programs. Specific programmatic interventions result in burdensome and costly regulations that have little effect on program quality. The National Institute of Education (September 19, 1977, p. 14), for example, found that:

> The language of the program development requirements is not "necessary" in the same sense as the funds allocation requirements. . . . Although local districts have many pressures to use funds more generally than the funds allocation regulations allow, they have little incentive to deliver inferior or ineffective services. Moreover, even if school districts follow the procedures established in the program development regulations, there is no guarantee that they will produce high-quality services. No regulations handed down from above can accomplish that.

Research on other federal programs reached similar conclusions; see, for example, Berman and McLaughlin, 1975; Rotberg, 1981; Wise, unpublished research; Hill et al., 1992.

Let's not fiddle with Chapter 1 in a way which waters down the funds for disadvantaged children and leads to funding abuses.

Ethel J. Lowry, State Chapter 1 Director

The government should, of course, take care not to provide *disincentives* to developing effective programs, for example, by focusing on tests of basic skills that encourage rote learning, creating regulations that can best be met by increasing student tracking, or creating uncoordinated, categorical programs that detract from the child's overall educational experience.

The discussion of pullout versus mainstream instruction provides an illustration of how precarious it would be for the federal government to attempt to intervene in programmatic matters. The commentaries we received demonstrated that either educational method can be done well or poorly. Judy Dierker, a teacher, wrote:

> I firmly believe the pullout model is the most effective and efficient. . . . It has been my experience, and that of the teachers I know, that the children pulled out for the Chapter 1 program are envied and other children beg to be allowed to come to Chapter 1. We have parents calling the schools requesting Chapter 1 help, and we have to deny their requests because the children are not eligible.[11]

In contrast, Richard L. Allington, a researcher, concluded:

> We see these at-risk children, regardless of categorical identification, spending large amounts of time in transition from one setting to the next, working with the least well-trained staff more often than with anyone else on the most poorly designed curriculum materials. We know that more often than not there is nothing special about the education offered in the special programs.[12]

Use a Separate Aid Program to Provide Incentives to Equalize Funding

The first two recommendations—increasing resources to the neediest communities and reformulating Chapter 1 to serve low-income children

---

[11]See Volume II of this report.
[12]Ibid.

at all achievement levels—can lead to significant improvements in the quality of education in poor communities. By themselves, however, improvements in Chapter 1 cannot address a more fundamental problem in U.S. public education: the large disparities in expenditures across school districts. As a practical matter, if the goal is to give the typical economically disadvantaged child in the United States greater (hence, compensatory) educational resources than the typical advantaged child, the federal government has to include some effort to equalize base expenditures.

The state and local financial disparities described above obviously hinder the achievement of federal goals for the education of low-income students. What might the federal government do to reduce these inequalities? Can Chapter 1, or other federal assistance, encourage school finance equalization among or within states?

One option is to use the current Chapter 2 Block Grant program, which is essentially general federal aid to education, as the base for a system of fiscal incentives for funding equalization within states. It appears feasible, with available data, to consider the implications of using Chapter 2 to encourage equalization and to analyze the costs and the political and legal context for school finance reform in each state. Such an analysis would provide the best basis for assessing both the potential effectiveness of incentives for equity and the likely distribution of the proposed incentive grants among states.

Given the current federal budget deficit, massive initial funding for equalization incentive grants would seem unrealistic. A demonstration program, however, could be phased in with relatively modest initial funding. For example, between $1 billion and $2 billion in equalization incentive grants might be distributed initially, rising to perhaps three or four times that much over a period of years. In this case, a gradual phase-in would serve the specific purpose of allowing the states time to take the difficult steps needed to equalize their systems before the stakes become too high.

Based on the following analysis, we conclude that the use of Chapter 2 for increasing the federal role in school finance equalization has advantages over alternative approaches. However, its feasibility as a major national program can be determined only by a demonstration that would provide information about how the incentive system would work in practice and about its associated costs and political implications. In the discussion below, we summarize a broader range of approaches for school finance equalization both among and within states and describe the Chapter 2 proposal in more detail.

Funding for schools must shift away from reliance on the local property tax.

Richard D. Miller, Director, Education Association

Equalization Among States

The federal government has limited options—and all are expensive ones—for reducing disparities in per pupil spending among states. The only real way to reduce present gaps in state spending is to fill them with (mainly) federal funds. With enough new federal money, education spending across the country could be made substantially more equal.

Remote as the prospects appear in the face of budget deficits, serious and powerful advocates of an active federal role have justified such funding on the grounds of equity, federalism, and common sense. The National Education Association, for example, has long espoused "one-third, one-third, and one-third" federal, state, and local funding.

Chapter 1 could set a good example by paying the same amount per formula child in every state, instead of giving the largest grants to states that already have the highest per pupil expenditure.

Wayne Teague,
Chief State School
Officer

Various bills to establish a program of general aid to education have been proposed in Congress since the 1970s, the most recent being the Fair Chance Act, introduced by Rep. Augustus F. Hawkins in 1990 (HR 3850, 101st Congress). This bill, which would have combined grants for inter-state equalization with incentives for intrastate equalization, called for the federal government to allocate aid to "move all States up to the level of funding the Secretary [of Education] determines to be necessary to as-sure a good education for all children."

Estimates of how much federal money would be required to equalize in-terstate finance vary dramatically, depending on the degree of equaliza-tion sought.[13] In 1989–1990, it would have taken approximately $10 bil-lion to bring per pupil expenditures in all the low-spending states up to the level of per pupil expenditures in the median state ($4357 in Colorado), excluding cost differentials. Three times that amount would have been required to bring every state up to the level of spending in Michigan ($5090), which in 1989–1990 spent more per pupil than three-quarters of the states.

Expenditures per pupil in the United States have been increasing at a rate of more than 5 percent per year. Thus, it would probably take about $12 billion and $35 billion, respectively, to achieve the Colorado and Michigan equalization standards in the 1993–1994 school year.

The lower-end estimate might appear feasible, certainly as a figure that might be attained after some years of federal intervention. The $12 bil-lion, after all, is less than double the amount now spent on Chapter 1 by itself. But the only reason these figures are not much higher is that they reflect the assumptions that (1) states already spending above the speci-fied target levels would get no aid and (2) the states receiving aid would use every new federal dollar to raise per pupil spending and none to

[13]See Volume III of this report. These estimates are calculated from data on enroll-ment and per pupil expenditure by state in National Center for Education Statistics (October 1992).

supplant funds from state or local sources. To the extent that such perfection in the targeting of federal aid proves unattainable, the cost would increase or the degree of equalization would decrease.

Equalization Within a State

The use of federal general-purpose grants to reward states for reducing fiscal disparities among local districts is a real possibility. Volume III describes three federal options for equalizing funding within states:

- Direct federal equalizing grants to districts.

- Federal pass-through grants to states—that is, grants that states will distribute to districts as needed to equalize spending.

- Federal incentives to states to equalize spending across their districts.

The first two options present various problems, most related to the realities of how local schools are financed in the United States, others related to technical considerations. The third option, however, offers real possibilities.

The federal government may be able to accomplish indirectly, through incentives, what it probably cannot do with either direct or pass-through aid, i.e., level disparities in per pupil expenditures among local school districts within states. Every state undoubtedly can equalize funding among its districts if it wants to. A number of states have done so to a substantial degree—some long ago, some recently; some voluntarily, others under court order.

Fiscal equalization is politically painful, however. It entails some combination of the redistribution of educational resources among communities and the imposition of higher taxes. Either can cut short the career of a state official. Therefore, federal incentives must be strong enough to overcome the costs to the states, or attractive enough to make redistribution palatable.

Three possibilities exist for encouraging intrastate equalization: (1) make some degree of equalization a prerequisite for Chapter 1 grants; (2) link the amount of a state's Chapter 1 aid to the degree of fiscal equality among its districts; and (3) use federal general education aid to states as the incentive for equalization.

The first two possibilities seem to contravene the goals of Chapter 1, although neither is as radical as it appears. Each, in fact, can be viewed as an extension to the state level of a Chapter 1 principle—comparability—long-established at the district level. Requiring equalization as a precondition for Chapter 1 grants would, in effect, elevate the comparability rule to the state level. In practice, imposing a statewide comparability

State and local governments are facing unprecedented fiscal crises that limit their ability to adequately meet the growing social service needs of poor families.

Arlene Zielke, Vice-President, Education Association

requirement would be almost equivalent to making Chapter 1 funding contingent on a specified degree of interdistrict fiscal equalization.[14]

The sudden imposition of a statewide comparability requirement without additional aid, however, would probably force some states out of the Chapter 1 program. States with large interdistrict disparities would have to spend several times as much as they receive under Chapter 1 to meet even a moderate equalization standard, an intolerable no-win situation for everyone—students, schools, districts, states, and the federal government. Moreover, Chapter 1 participants, already disadvantaged by unevenly distributed base expenditures, would be harmed further if federal funds were withdrawn.

The third approach—a general aid proposal linked to equalization—in contrast to the first two, has much to recommend it. With general aid, the federal government would possess genuine leverage in encouraging intrastate equalization. By distributing general aid in amounts linked to intrastate equalization, the government could simultaneously promote equity within states and provide resources for, say, efforts to raise the quality of schools.

Although general aid would not be earmarked for particular purposes, states could view it as a federal contribution to the cost of equalization. And because the aid would be unrestricted, states would value each dollar of general aid more highly than a dollar of categorical aid. The incentive effect per dollar would be correspondingly stronger. Free of concern that disadvantaged students might be adversely affected, the government could set both the stakes and the degree of equalization higher.[15] More states might receive offers that they considered "too good to refuse."

A general aid incentive approach has the major advantage of assigning functions to federal and state government that each is well qualified to perform. The federal government would allocate funds and set equity standards. The state would decide how best to reduce disparities among its own districts. In contrast, any plan for direct or pass-through equalization aid to school districts would require the federal government to involve itself in the details of state school finance systems—a task for which it is poorly equipped.

---

[14]It is "almost equivalent" because a statewide comparability rule would apply only to expenditure levels in Chapter 1 schools, not to expenditure levels of whole districts. In practice, however, this would be a distinction without a difference because a large percentage of all schools currently are Chapter 1 schools. Although, in theory, a state could bring up only the Chapter 1 schools to stipulated comparability standards, to do so would be to create a two-class system in many school districts, leaving the non-Chapter 1 minority of schools funded at lower levels. Such a pattern would not prevail for long.

[15]Equity standards (i.e., the degree of equalization sought) and measures (i.e., assessing compliance with the standards) are discussed in Volume III.

A system of federal incentive grants for intrastate equalization could be structured in various ways. We are not prepared at this time to recommend any particular design, nor do we claim to have worked out the technical details. For purposes of illustration, however, we offer the following example of how incentive grants might work.

Assume that the Chapter 2 grant program, with three or four times its present appropriation of about $500 million dollars per year, becomes the base on which incentives for intrastate equalization would be built. This program provides a possible statutory foundation on which to establish a fiscally equalizing general aid program and a concrete illustration of how such a program might work.

Currently, Chapter 2 Block Grant funds are allocated among states in proportion to each state's school-age (5–17) population. Suppose, for the moment, that the same formula is used to allocate incentive grants. The major difference, however, is that under the current Chapter 2 program the formula determines the actual amount of aid that a state receives, whereas under the proposed incentive grant program, it would determine the *maximum* amount of aid that a state could *earn*.

The percentage of this maximum that a state actually received would depend on the degree of inequality in education spending per pupil among the state's school districts. States with the most highly equalized districts would receive the maximum grants, calculated from the formula; states with less equitable financing systems would receive only fractions of the maximum grants, calculated according to a sliding scale. Those with the most egregious disparities might receive no aid at all.

The federal government must seek ways of compensating for unequal education funding.

Sheila Slater, Teacher

These incentive grants would be considered general-purpose federal education aid to the states. They would not be earmarked for particular uses or beneficiaries, nor would states be obliged to account for their use or to distribute them in any particular manner to school districts. The intent is that each state would add the federal funds to the state funds that it distributes as general state aid to local school districts.

The federal dollars would be counted fully, in the same manner as state and local dollars, in measuring the degree of fiscal equity among a state's school districts. The federal government might reasonably attach such provisions as a strong maintenance-of-effort requirement to encourage the states to use the federal aid to supplement state and local education funds. Such provisions, however, would be incidental rather than essential to the purpose of encouraging states to equalize their school finance systems.

The most critical and sensitive element of any such incentive mechanism would be the indicator, or set of indicators, used to quantify the degree of fiscal inequality among the districts of each state. Candidate indicators abound. The past 20 years of school finance research have produced a large literature on measurement of school finance equity and an arsenal of specific equity statistics (Berne and Stiefel, 1984).

The possibilities range from crude measures that reflect nothing more than the difference in spending between a state's highest-spending and lowest-spending districts to sophisticated indexes that take into account the whole distribution of per pupil spending, as well as adjust for differences in district size, pupil composition, and unit cost. The problem, if anything, is an overabundance of choices. Moreover, each measure tends to yield a different rating of relative equity by state and consequently would lead to a somewhat different distribution of the federal equalizing grants.

The equity indicator, therefore, should be chosen carefully, taking account of the implications of each possible choice. Congress might even want to build multiple equity indicators into the formula (the additional complexity notwithstanding) in the interest of fairness to states with different patterns of funds distribution among their districts.

To avoid unfairness, the formula might exclude certain education expenditures from the calculations and allow adjustments for certain district characteristics. For instance, excluding expenditure for pupil transportation would make the formula fairer, as would adjusting the data to take into account the almost unavoidably high per pupil outlays of very small districts.

Decisions would also have to be made about the legitimacy and the appropriate means of adjusting for interdistrict differences in percentages of costly-to-serve pupils and in the prices of educational resources. In general, the formula might appropriately exclude funds derived from federal categorical grants from the equity calculations, but it should definitely include funds derived from federal general-purpose grants, such as Impact Aid or the equalization aid being discussed here.

A critical consideration in designing an incentive formula would be the "steepness" of the relationship between equity and federal aid. For instance, should the state with the worst equity rating receive 80 percent, 50 percent, or 20 percent as much aid as a state with an average rating (other things being equal), or should it receive no aid at all? Because the proposed federal rewards for equalization would be relatively small, it is important to maximize the incentive effect per dollar. This argues for a formula that gives little or no aid to states with large interdistrict disparities but that offers the largest possible rewards to states that substantially enhance equity.

The effectiveness of federal aid in leveling the existing intrastate disparities in per pupil spending clearly will vary by state. In some states, the cost of eliminating large interdistrict disparities may well dwarf the potential federal rewards, rendering the incentives ineffective. In such cases, however, the cost to the federal government could be minimal, provided that the formula is designed to give little aid to inequitable states.

In other cases, however, federal aid might tip the balance, inducing states that would not have done so to adopt major school finance reforms. This outcome would be particularly likely where other pressures—political or judicial—are already being exerted in favor of school finance equity.

One final point: The foregoing discussion has focused on the use of federal funds to promote intrastate fiscal equity, but if substantial federal funds were made available for that purpose, such funds could also be used to reduce interstate disparities The federal government therefore might consider distributing funds so as to promote both objectives simultaneously.

To promote both objectives, the government might determine each state's maximum grant not according to the Chapter 2 formula but according to a formula that takes state fiscal capacity into account. For example, if aid were inversely related to state per capita income, the formula would boost spending in the lower-income, lower-spending states.

Although the distribution of incentive grants in this manner is not unreasonable, it might entail a trade-off between interstate and intrastate equalization. Some of the least equitable states are also high-spending states. If the grants that these states could earn were reduced in the interest of interstate equalization, the incentives for interdistrict equalization would also be weakened. Congress would have to consider carefully, therefore, the relative importance that it attaches to each equalization goal.

The effectiveness of incentives would depend directly on the size of the potential rewards. The Chapter 2 Block Grant program is a logical place to start. Chapter 2 is essentially general federal aid, and it could readily be amended to increase its size and tie state receipt of funds to the degree of intrastate equalization.

Young people cannot be denied an education because they happen to live in a poor area. Otherwise, we will continue to be a "nation at risk."

Gaynor McCown, Teacher

5. PROGRAM ACCOUNTABILITY AND ACHIEVEMENT TESTING

Section 4 of this report called for enriching the educational experience of low-income children of all achievement levels by increasing funding for the nation's lowest-income districts and thereby facilitating the adoption of schoolwide projects. If these changes are to be effective, a new concept of accountability in Chapter 1 is also required.

In a sense, policymakers need to consider anew the perennial question that has accompanied Chapter 1 since 1965: How will the federal government—and the schools—know whether what they are doing is accomplishing anything?

Program accountability in education was almost an invention of Title I/Chapter 1. Senator Robert F. Kennedy added an evaluation requirement to the original Title I legislation in 1965. His amendment, written out of his concern that federal education money would disappear without a trace in local school budgets, sought to ensure that parents and citizens would know how well they were served by the new federal assistance. Almost immediately, the evaluation requirement took on a life of its own, with two distinct approaches.

The first approach involved national evaluations of Chapter 1, as well as studies that provided a more general sense of trends in the education of low-income students. The research included information about (1) resources and educational programs in low-income schools and (2) student attainment, including test scores, grades, promotion rates, attendance rates, high school graduation, and college attendance. The best of this research has served the education community well in the past and can be expected to continue to provide essential information both about the effectiveness of Chapter 1 and about trends in the education of low-income students more generally.

The second approach consisted of annual programs of achievement testing at the local level for purposes of accountability. For reasons described below, we conclude that this approach has had adverse consequences and should be replaced by accountability methods that are more consistent with the reformulation of Chapter 1 recommended in this report.

Current Testing Practices

Conventional wisdom holds that testing can help to improve schools: Test children and they will learn. In fact, Chapter 1 from the outset has

[With schoolwide programs] there would be no treatment and control group; there would be only served students.

Joy Frechtling, Senior Associate, Research Organization

We have watched students who know they can't read the [test] items attempt to comply by filling in the circles and crying while doing so.

Victoria Temple Meyer, Psychologist

encouraged the testing of participating children. As the 1990s dawned, testing permeated virtually every aspect of the program. Students are tested first to determine program eligibility and, at the end of the year, to see how much they have learned. Schools are also required to assess the progress of Chapter 1 participants in the regular instructional program and in basic and more advanced skills.

If only the Department of Defense were as regulated as Chapter 1.

Stanley J. Herman, Associate Superintendent of Schools

Tests are employed to make distinctions between students at the 20th percentile in reading in fifth grade and at the 10th in second grade. They are used to determine whether the school should offer mathematics, or language arts, or English as a second language, and if so in which grades. Many national assessments have relied on tests—either aggregating existing test results or administering special tests as part of the assessment. And school districts must contribute the data from their testing efforts to such national assessments by aggregating test scores and providing them to the Title I Evaluation and Reporting System (TIERS) designed to capture nationally comparable data.

Finally, tests serve as the essential accountability mechanism in the "program improvement" provisions of Chapter 1. These provisions authorize school district and even state intervention in poorly performing schools. In fact, schools are required to evaluate student achievement on an annual cycle, with fall-to-fall or spring-to-spring testing, not fall-to spring testing. In policy terms, policymakers hope that the more they hold schools accountable for the test scores of Chapter 1 students, the more their educational programs will improve.

The federal programs, so essential in Kentucky to educational equity and excellence, unfortunately have discouraged the use of authentic assessment.

Lois Adams-Rodgers, State Deputy Commissioner

Despite the fact that RAND's request for commentary on Chapter 1 gave little attention to testing, many respondents commented on it. Few of the commentaries had anything positive to say about current testing practices. The proliferation of testing has led to a diverse set of problems and negative incentives:

1. Chapter 1 testing encourages the teaching of a narrow set of measurable skills.

Many commentators believe that Chapter 1 testing discourages the teaching of higher-order skills and subjects that the tests do not cover. This trend clearly contravenes the broader educational goals of effective education programs and the 1988 Hawkins-Stafford amendments, both of which encourage greater emphasis on higher-order cognitive skills. Most multiple-choice tests used to assess Chapter 1 (and school programs more generally) encourage drill and practice, rote memorization, and reduced attention to such subjects as social studies, science, and writing, which the tests do not emphasize.

Testimony on February 19, 1992, before the Subcommittee on Elementary, Secondary, and Vocational Education, Committee on Education and Labor, U.S. House of Representatives, concluded that

> [Test-based accountability] has been tried many times over a period of centuries in numerous countries, and its track record is unimpressive. Most recently, it was the linchpin of the educational reform movement of the 1980s, the failure of which provides much of the impetus for the current wave of reform. . . . Holding people accountable for performance on tests tends to narrow the curriculum. It inflates test scores, leading to phony accountability. It can have pernicious effects on instruction, such as substitution of cramming for teaching. Evidence also indicates that it can adversely affect students already at risk—for example, increasing the dropout rate and producing more egregious cramming for the tests in schools with large minority enrollments (Koretz et al., 1992).

These conclusions were confirmed by a recent study which pointed out the negative consequence of the current emphasis on "high-stakes" testing. Such testing is used particularly in classrooms with high proportions of low-income and minority children, many of whom receive Chapter 1 services.

> [T]here is more reliance on mandated test scores in high-minority classrooms than in low-minority classrooms. Teachers of high-minority classes report more test pressure and test-oriented instruction than teachers of low-minority classes. Yet such teachers do not believe that these testing programs benefit curriculum, instruction, or learning. . . . These results suggest a gap in instructional emphasis between high and low-minority classrooms that conflict with our national concern for equity in the quality of education (Madaus et al., 1992).

A teacher sums it up this way:

> We are preparing a generation of robots. Kids are learning exclusively through rote. We have children who are given no conceptual framework. They do not learn to think, because their teachers are straitjacketed by tests that measure only isolated skills. As a result, they can be given no electives, nothing wonderful or fanciful or beautiful, nothing that touches the spirit or the soul. Is this what the country wants for its black children (Kozol, 1992)?

2. The use of test scores for funds allocation often results in less funding for schools that make achievement gains.

In addition to assessing school performance, test scores are often used to determine Chapter 1 funding. The current reliance on "gain" scores works against schools that have strong programs in the early years or promote successful students out of Chapter 1. Indeed, increases in test scores, whatever the reason, might result in diminished Chapter 1 funding.

The school's success became a barrier to continuing the program that worked so well.

LaVaun Dennett, Former Principal

Elfrieda H. Hiebert, a university-based researcher wrote: "Punishment for a job well done defeats the purpose of Chapter 1."[1] She described a Rube Goldberg system of rules and regulations in effect at the local level that caught teachers coming and going. That is clearly not the intent of the program, of its authors, or even of the people managing the program at the local level. But the complexities of administering it in some situations are a never-ending catch-22. As Hiebert pointed out:

> The success of the children on the standardized test turned out to have unhappy consequences. The guidelines from the state Chapter 1 agency emphasize services for the schools with the lowest test scores. One of the particpating schools lost part of an FTE [full-time equivalent], which went to one of the nonparticipating schools. . . . The schools were also punished in another way. Since the majority of children in the bottom quartile had learned to read [in a Chapter 1 program] as first graders, [they] received fewer Chapter 1 places as second graders. . . . There was concern about explaining to the state Chapter 1 office the decision to serve second graders at the 25–30 NCE [normal curve equivalent] level when fifth graders at the 20 NCE were not served.[2]

3. Test score changes from year to year, or from school to school, tell little about the quality of the educational program.

When evaluation techniques are not commensurate with instructional methods, teachers become demoralized.

Gerald W. Bracey, Education Consultant

The quality of an education system, of individual schools, or of a specific program—e.g., Chapter 1—cannot be measured simply by comparing test score fluctuations from one year to another, or by comparing schools or classrooms on test scores. The results cannot account for changes in student population in a particular school, incentives for encouraging certain students to take (or not to take) the test, or the consistency or lack of it between the test and the instructional program.

Tests clearly cannot separate out the effects of the Chapter 1 program, which accounts for less than 7 percent of a student's instructional time, from the overall instructional experience. Anyone who has tried to collate and interpret the test score submissions from school districts throughout the country knows that these tests have merely created administrative burdens and paperwork that are unrelated to educational benefits, although they obviously contribute to rising educational costs.

4. Alternatives to these tests do not exist.

Even accepting the assumption that students, and their teachers, do a better job if held accountable for test scores, one might question how tests that have little to do with broader educational goals can create the

---

[1] See Volume II of this report.
[2] Ibid.

appropriate incentives. There is little disagreement about the negative aspects of multiple-choice, standardized tests.

According to one argument, however, testing can be improved by developing innovative new tests, often called "authentic tests," which would include performance assessments, essay exams, and portfolio assessments. Little attention is paid to how long such tests would take to develop, how much they would cost and, indeed, whether they could be administered on a large scale, particularly for purposes of national accountability.

Edward J. Meade, Jr., formerly with the Ford Foundation, raised the issue of whether the costs of testing had not risen far beyond their benefit:

> I have been concerned for some time that the need for program evaluation and accountability (certainly legitimate) has sometimes—in some cases, often—been the tail that wags the Chapter 1 dog. For starters, I'd be pleased to have you study the costs (real and contributed) for evaluation and accountability at the local district, state, and federal levels. . . . Sometimes, I think we spend more time, effort, and resources to evaluate than we do to improve that which is being evaluated.[3]

In short, authentic assessment for all Chapter 1 schools does not now exist. Moreover, it would be expensive to develop and administer, although it might be useful for research or diagnostic purposes.

5. Quite apart from the detrimental effects of testing on individual students and classrooms, the use of such tests to trigger school district and state intervention in poorly performing schools is questionable.

The 1988 Hawkins-Stafford amendments added new provisions to encourage program improvement and greater accountability. In general, Chapter 1 programs deemed to need improvement are those in which aggregate achievement scores of participating students show either no change or a decline over the course of a year. Districts are required to intervene to upgrade performance in such schools. Following district intervention, states are authorized to help design and implement joint state-district improvement plans for schools that continue to show no improvement.

Schools would be encouraged to experiment with alternative practices if the reliance on tests for program improvement identification were removed.

Merwin L. Smith, State Chapter 1 Administrator

By the 1991–1992 school year, 10,582 schools in all 50 states had been identified as needing improvement (U.S. Department of Education, June 1992). Six out of ten were in the first year of program improvement; 33 percent in the second year; and 6 percent in the third. Not surprisingly, schools in high-poverty districts (those in which 21 percent of the population are poor) were three times as likely to be in the program improve-

---

[3]Ibid.

ment category as schools in low-poverty districts (those in which less than 7 percent of the population are poor).

Unfortunately, the tests that determine the need for program improvement are inherently unreliable and therefore not well suited for the intended purpose. In the nationally representative Chapter 1 Implementation Study, about one-half of identified schools "tested out" of program improvement in the second year without making any changes in their Chapter 1 programs (Millsap et al., 1992). The scores improved because of a variety of circumstances that could not be identified. Test scores tend to fluctuate so much from year to year—apart from changes in the quality of education—that many schools identified as requiring program improvement apparently did nothing but wait until the next testing period, successfully counting on "testing out" of the requirements.

These findings do not mitigate the importance of district or state assistance to "failing" schools. They do, however, point out the impracticality of mandating this intervention nationwide based on test scores.

An Alternative Approach to Accountability

While most observers agree on the negative consequences of current testing practices, some conclude that (1) accountability requirements can serve to encourage higher performance and (2) better tests—for example, tests that emphasize reasoning and problem solving—might have a positive effect on teaching methods. These arguments clearly have some validity.

The evidence from both research and practical experience suggests, however, that federal testing requirements do not lead to improvements in education. This conclusion also applies to recent proposals to increase Chapter 1 accountability requirements as a trade-off for reducing other regulations. Unfortunately, the proposals cannot be implemented without continuing to incur the negative consequences of current testing practices.

Indeed, increased pressure to measure performance is likely to have the same result as in England: testing on a massive scale, recently brought to a halt by the "rebellion" of teachers, principals, and parents. A recent study concluded that:

> The attempt in Britain to define attainment targets and measure them using "authentic" assessment tasks at the individual student level at age 7 has serious implications for the upcoming re-authorization of Chapter 1. A host of technical and managerial problems arose with the SATs [Standard Attainment Tasks] at key stage 1.... Further, the SATs were judged to define what was to be taught and learned in ways that went against the grain of good early childhood practice.... Proposals in the

United States to assess all Chapter 1 students at grade 1 and again at grade 4 using "authentic" assessment techniques carry with them the same sorts of technical and managerial problems associated with the key stage 1 assessment in England, and run the same danger of producing similar effects on instruction (Kellaghan and Madaus, 1993).

Accountability requirements were included in the original Title I legislation to provide information about whether or not the money was being spent wisely. The negative effects of the requirements could not be foreseen at that time. However, after 25 years of experience showing that test scores tell little about the quality of the educational program—and at the same time have adverse consequences—we conclude that it is counterproductive to continue to require them.

We recommend, therefore, that federal requirements for Chapter 1 testing—either for purposes of accountability or for determining student or school eligibility for program participation—be eliminated. Chapter 1 students should take the same tests routinely given to other children in their school district.

Chapter 1 should have the same curriculum standards as other programs.

Patricia E. Lucas, Principal

In reality, no testing program can separate the effects of Chapter 1—currently 3 percent of total funding for elementary and secondary education—from the effects of either the overall education experience or the broader environment. School districts and states have many pressures for educational accountability; the choice of specific measures can best be left to local discretion. Moreover, the proposal advanced in Section 4 to provide services to a wider range of low-income children should relieve much of the pressure for achievement testing for selection purposes.

Federal testing requirements, if eliminated for program accountability and student eligibility, would cease to influence the educational program in low-income schools, encourage the teaching of a narrow set of skills, and create perverse incentives that punish schools for raising achievement. Other accountability mechanisms can be created to encourage improved performance at the local level.

Schoolwide improvement programs not based on failure or low achievement alone would inspire school personnel to evaluate student development on more than standardized tests.

Kenwood N. Nordquist, Principal

Chapter 1 is a remarkably complicated accountability problem. The transaction involves many actors, including the federal government, state government, school district, school, parents, and students. Although schools perform the activity at the encouragement of the federal government (which is in a position to affect the school's benefits), the real beneficiaries are students, with no real capacity to affect the school one way or the other.

Probably the best place to start rethinking accountability in Chapter 1 can be found in the existing Program Improvement provisions. As de-

Incentives can be provided for improving the percentage of students who graduate and the percentage who go on to college and remain there.

Ramon C. Cortines,
Superintendent of
Schools

scribed above, these provisions depend almost exclusively on student testing to identify schools potentially in need of district or state intervention.

Program Improvement should be amended to include a far broader array of measures. These might include (1) indicators of student performance and progress, for example, grades, attendance, promotions, and dropout rates; and (2) information about the school's educational program as shown, for example, by course offerings, class size, and teacher qualifications. The choice of specific measures should be left to the discretion of states and localities, which have the best information both about the availability of data and the measures that would most closely reflect the districts' educational program.

Chapter 1 schools could provide this information to district officials, who would, in turn, report to state Chapter 1 officials. This approach, combined with national studies and evaluations, would provide valuable information to all involved with Chapter 1: Federal policymakers could draw on the results of national evaluations to gauge the effectiveness of the national effort; elected federal officials would be alerted to significant progress or problems in schools in their own constituencies; state officials would have statewide access to district reports; school district officials would have much richer information on operations in their own Chapter 1 schools and the problems these schools face; and parents and community leaders would be in a position to judge how well their local schools were doing.

The ideas for our project were not based solely on students' test results, but came from parents, teachers, and administrators as well.

Michael Citro,
Principal

The accountability system proposed here pretends neither that achievement data alone are adequate for accountability nor that local accountability processes can be counted on without state or federal oversight. It is based on the evidence that tested achievement by itself is an inadequate measure of program performance (and hence an unreliable ally of accountability) and that accountability at the local level is often nonexistent, inadequate, or fragmented.

State oversight, with federal assistance, is needed. But from their distant vantage points, neither the federal government nor even the states can guarantee local accountability. A system is needed that encourages accountability and better information at the local level.

Districts should be responsible for taking remedial action toward their most troubled schools. Remedies might include, for example, increased funding, enriched staffing, staff development, new equipment, or closure and development of a "new" school. They should be school-specific and take account of special circumstances, such as high student turnover or rapid demographic change. States would then become responsible for monitoring local procedures, providing assistance as required, and stepping in, if necessary.[4]

---

[4]This discussion of federal accountability mechanisms draws on Paul T. Hill et al. (1992), and Paul T. Hill and Josephine J. Bonan (1991).

6. MYTHS AND REALITIES

Despite the growing severity of the problems Chapter 1 was designed to address, the program has not been modified to respond to the realities of increased poverty and vast differences in educational expenditures between rich and poor school districts. Part of the reason is budgetary: Since 1980, the federal budget has become a fiscal nightmare in which entitlement spending (i.e., spending mandated by law for Social Security and for health care), defense spending, interest on the national debt, and lowered taxation have created unprecedented pressure on other federal spending, including such programs as Chapter 1.

We must ask Congress to use the peace dividend to support one of the most needed and successful education programs in the nation.

Paul D. Houston, School Superintendent

Federal budget problems have, in turn, raised the financial pressure on state and local governments, which provide the lion's share of education funding. All three entities have had to deal with a common problem: Sluggish economic growth and two recessions in the past 12 years have simultaneously lowered tax revenues while raising mandated expenditures for such programs as unemployment compensation and health care.

Myths About Education

In this difficult fiscal environment, certain beliefs—myths, really—about educational performance in low-income areas have further weakened effective federal efforts to reform and improve Chapter 1.

The first myth is that federal education programs do not work. This is the most destructive myth of all because it is so succinctly stated and easy to understand, and, if true, it would destroy the entire rationale for Chapter 1.

But the myth is demonstrably false. National evaluations of Chapter 1 show that the students are making gains in basic skills. Moreover, despite the public outcry about American education, we found no evidence that student achievement has declined in the past generation. The educational system may not be performing as well as people have a right to expect. But it is probably performing at least as well as it did a generation ago. With respect to minority children, prime targets for Chapter 1, the National Assessment of Educational Progress reports achievement gains:

> [While] White students consistently had higher average achievement than their Black and Hispanic counterparts . . . the trends . . . indicate considerable improvement by both minority groups. . . . [For example,] in mathematics, the only significant progress by White students since 1973 was at age 9. In comparison, Black students showed significant improvement at all three ages, as did Hispanic students at ages 9 and 13. The reading results show the same pattern. Although the proficiency of

White 17-year-olds has improved significantly since 1971, 9- and 13-year-olds were reading at about the same level in 1990 as nearly two decades ago. Black students, however, demonstrated significantly higher proficiency in 1990 at all three ages. Hispanic students also showed gains at age 17, yet their reading performance did not change significantly at the younger ages (National Center for Education Statistics, 1991).

Recognition, perks, reduced class size, and money need to be provided to recruit and keep the best teachers.

GwenCarol
H. Holmes,
Teacher

The second myth, a corollary of the first, holds that the nation cannot solve educational problems by throwing money at them. That is true only if one assumes that offering poor children the opportunities routinely available to their more affluent peers is the same as throwing money at a problem. Teachers' expertise and class size do matter (see, for example, Ferguson, 1991).

Clearly, some schools—rich and poor alike—use money more productively than others. However, without adequate funding, even the best intentions cannot reduce student-teacher ratios, or support essential tutorial programs for small groups of students. Nor can underfunded school systems attract the best teachers. Teaching salaries influence teachers' career decisions—whether they will teach for one year only, or for long enough to gain expertise. Salaries also have an influence on where teachers choose to teach. And because, all things being equal, teachers prefer districts with high socioeconomic status (SES), low-income districts need to pay higher salaries to attract the best teachers. (See, for example, Ferguson, 1991, and Murnane, 1991.)

> This evidence suggests that if school districts choose wisely, higher salaries will result in higher quality teachers. Thus, the evidence of the impact of money on the career decisions of teachers and potential teachers supports the view that funding levels influence a district's ability to staff its schools with skilled teachers (Murnane, 1991).

The conditions in low-income schools described above—overcrowded classrooms, inexperienced teachers, shortages of counselors, science laboratories that lack Bunsen burners or microscopes, forced rationing of compensatory services, decaying facilities—cannot be alleviated without additional resources. A judge in a school finance case put it this way: "If money is inadequate to improve education, the residents of poor districts should at least have an equal opportunity to be disappointed by its failure" (Kozol, 1992).[1]

---

[1]Over the past 30 years, a large number of studies have been conducted to identify relationships between school expenditures and student achievement. (See, for example, Ferguson, 1991; Finn and Achilles, 1990; Hanushek, 1991; Murnane, 1991; Odden, 1990; Pate-Bain et al., 1992; and Shapson et al., 1980.) Teacher expertise emerges as the most significant predictor, with class size showing positive results in a smaller number of studies. Overall, the results of the studies are quite ambiguous: Some results are positive, others negative; some studies show no clear trends. It is not surprising that this research—generally, large-scale statistical reanalyses of questionable data bases—is difficult to interpret.

First, it is often not possible to control for the crucial variables, e.g., SES, that overwhelm the educational experience. In many cases, the quality of the educational experience

The third misconception holds that low-income children actually receive, when one counts in diverse special categorical programs, more funding, and hence more educational services, than do most other youngsters. Therefore, the argument goes, why aren't these students making more dramatic achievement gains?

In many jurisdictions, this criticism amounts to little more than a denial of reality: Large differences in education expenditures exist *even after the addition of Chapter 1 funds*. As this report makes clear, the Chapter 1 program does not provide anything close to the level of funds needed to compensate for the large inequalities in resources between low-income and more affluent districts. Indeed, Barro drew three conclusions after reviewing Chapter 1 expenditure patterns:[2]

---

cannot be separated from the characteristics of the students—a problem exacerbated by the fact that student SES, school expenditures, and program quality are highly correlated. The highest-income students have access to the best educational programs. Variables are confounded in other ways—for example, the lowest-achieving children may receive special instruction in small classes, thereby negating any potential positive relationship between small class size and student achievement.

Second, because most of the studies reanalyze existing data collected for other purposes, the data tend to be low-quality, incomplete, and limited in size and scope. Moreover, for some variables, the range may be quite narrow—for example, few studies of class size can identify the effects of either very small or very large classes.

Third, the measurement problems are severe. School district budgets are difficult to interpret or to track to the school level. Therefore, expenditure data provide little information about how the funds are actually used in schools, or even the proportion of funds used for instructional purposes. Some seemingly high-spending districts may need to spend a relatively large proportion of their funds on transportation, security, or social service costs. Measurement of student performance is also tenuous. The traditional standardized tests are limited in scope and may bear little resemblance to the educational program in particular schools. In short, there is no way for large statistical analyses, using highly imprecise measures, to determine which students took or did not take the test, what their educational experiences were (e.g., whether they had access to the best teachers or to the smallest classes), and whether the standardized tests accurately reflected the content of the educational programs.

Because the studies are ambiguous and because some schools use resources more productively than others, the school-finance reform movement is placing increased emphasis on monitoring school districts' use of funds, and on assessing the success of school finance remedies, at least in part, by students' scores on standardized tests. The rationale—encouraging the wise use of funds—is clear. What is less clear is whether (for reasons discussed in Section 4, in the subsection "Limitations of the Federal Role," and Section 5, above) an increased emphasis on overseeing educational programs or testing students will have the desired effect. In practice, these well-intended remedies may run the risk of creating greater increases in bureaucracy and paperwork than in educational quality. Ferguson (1991) describes it this way: "Forcing all districts to comply with any uniform set of spending rules or spending levels would be very risky business—probably impossible to administer successfully. This is because schools have different demands on their resources (e.g., necessary maintenance and transportation expenditures vary greatly), because standard practices often include expenditures that are inefficient but difficult to regulate from above (e.g., schools apparently overspend on administration and reduce class sizes below typically optimal levels, but they may sometimes have good reasons), and because the number and quality of teachers that a district can attract depend not only on the salary it pays but also on the salaries that surrounding districts and other professions pay."

[2]See Volume III of this report.

- First, there is substantial inequality in regular education spending both among and within states. Often the differences in base expenditure among jurisdictions are larger than the Chapter 1 funds available per participant.

- Second, Chapter 1 funds are not distributed in a way that affects disparities in base expenditure. At the state level, Chapter 1 funding actually adds to the disparities in base expenditure; at the local level, it is neutral.

- Finally, the federal government now has no other education policy in place to reduce interstate or intrastate fiscal disparities.

The final myth, an effort to avoid the self-evident, proposes that schools can be reformed without new resources in low-income areas and without also dealing with problems in surrounding communities. Indeed, the educational problems in low-income schools cannot be separated from the problems of poverty and unemployment in the larger society. In recent years, several proposals—the restructuring of schools, the introduction of vouchers, and the use of national standards and national testing—have been put forward as the reforms needed to strengthen the nation's education system. Neither individually nor collectively do they respond to the problems of low-income schools.

Our nation's provision of Chapter 1 resources expresses commitment to the belief that schools can make a difference.

Carolyn Hughes Chapman, Professor

By focusing attention on reform proposals that appear to provide an easy solution, typically with little additional funding, the nation may fail to make the hard choices required to address serious and difficult problems in low-income areas. As one observer put it: "Amidst the cymbals and the drums, the hype and the sound bites, [teachers] know that at the end of the day they will be teaching 30 children in a classroom (perhaps 150 per day in a secondary school)" (Eisner, 1992). Without major increases in the resources available to low-income schools, teachers in these areas will continue to face the same reality, whatever becomes of today's reform proposals.

Reforming Chapter 1

Policymakers, analysts, educators, and the public need to move beyond the comfort of these myths and misconceptions and address forthrightly the real issues involved in providing high-quality education in our poorest communities. The time has come to act on the promise of improving the education of low-income students—the promise that the federal government first enunciated in 1965.

- The first issue is financial: Schools serving many of these students need more resources.

- The second is a matter of focus: Federal funds should be directed to the areas with the largest concentration of these youngsters.

- The third issue involves educational and policy coherence: If a critical mass of resources is available, Chapter 1 can play a much more significant role in improving education in the country's poorest communities by encouraging schoolwide improvement.

The basic purpose of Chapter 1 was always to provide resources to schools serving large proportions of low-income youngsters; it should be reoriented around the needs of these young people, not diluted at the school level by comparing students on test results because resources are available to serve only a small proportion of the student body.

Most evaluations of the existing Chapter 1 program do an excellent job of assessing Chapter 1 on its own terms. But in fact, these analyses have contributed to the nation's inability to examine federal compensatory programs in a larger context. Researchers can examine the details of how Chapter 1 funds filter their way down to individual districts, schools, and classrooms. They can calculate the number of extra minutes of instruction purchased each day by Chapter 1. They can suggest how to improve the existing program, on the assumption that funding levels remain constant.

Chapter 1 has a long history of "bean counting."

Lorin W. Anderson, Professor

Unfortunately, these analyses, however detailed and helpful, miss the forest for the trees. The "forest" described in this report has three major markers: Resources in most low-income schools and districts are generally inadequate; the additional resources provided by Chapter 1 are not sufficient to make the program effective nationally as a stand-alone effort; and the environment for Chapter 1 is today far more challenging than the problems for which the program was originally designed.

Even under the best of circumstances, Chapter 1 services can rarely be better than the schools in which they are offered. In affluent school districts—those with very few low-income students and substantial revenues from a healthy local property base—federal assistance obviously helps to provide supplemental instruction for low-achieving students, even though such districts could probably find the resources themselves. In these districts, the Chapter 1 effort generally can build on a high resource base and effective schools to deliver services that will likewise be of high quality.

In moderate-income communities, including those with a significant number of low-income students and students from "working poor" families, the current Chapter 1 conception probably fits its task reasonably well. These districts are not wealthy. They have to stretch to provide high-quality education services. Without Chapter 1, the low-income students attending schools in these communities could easily fall between the cracks.

Schools cannot solve the educational problem independently of the rest of society.

E. G. Sherburne, Jr., Education Consultant

But schools in the poorest-of-the-poor school districts—in rural Appalachia, in the Mississippi delta, in the nation's inner cities—are often in appalling shape. In many, the physical facilities are seriously decayed, sometimes unsafe. Others have several classes, sometimes as many as four or five, crammed into the same room, or offer remedial programs in hallways.

We'd better find ways of improving living conditions for all poor people, if not for charitable reasons, then for the hope of living in a peaceful society.

Richard A. Denoyer, School Superintendent

Dropout rates are alarming; although district officials deplore the dropout rate, principals and teachers find themselves counting on it to bring class size down to manageable proportions by midyear. Lead-based paint peels from walls. Laboratories are unequipped. Classes in music, art, or drama are unavailable; if sought, they are dismissed as frills. These schools are suffering from financial starvation.

In these schools, Chapter 1 is a crucial resource offering some flexibility as administrators and teachers try to cope with the most critical aspects of the crisis. But under current constraints Chapter 1 is not enough. Chapter 1 can provide essential supplemental services, but it is no substitute for the fundamental improvements that schools require.

Up until now, the nation has chosen not to make the needed investment in low-income schools. Under the circumstances, policymakers should be realistic about what can and cannot be accomplished by rhetoric about world-class standards, accountability, or choice. Setting vague and unrealistic goals, or constructing additional tests, does not substitute for high quality education. We will not produce better schools—no matter what peripheral reforms are implemented—unless we address the serious underfunding of education in poor communities. Further delays will result in diminished opportunities for this generation of low-income children.

REFERENCES

Barro, S. M. (1991). *The Distribution of Federal Elementary-Secondary Education Grants Among the States.* Washington, D.C.: U.S. Department of Education, Office of Policy and Planning.

Berman, P., and M. McLaughlin (1975, April). *Federal Programs Supporting Educational Change, Vol. 4: Findings and Review.* Santa Monica, Calif.: RAND, R-1589/4-HEW.

Berne, R., and L. Stiefel (1984). *The Measurement of Equity in School Finance.* Baltimore, Md.: The Johns Hopkins Press.

Blank, Rolf K. (1989, September). "Educational Effects of Magnet High Schools." Paper prepared for Conference on Choice and Control in American Education, Madison: University of Wisconsin.

Carter, L. F. (1983). *A Study of Compensatory and Elementary Education: The Sustaining Effects Study.* Washington, D.C.: U.S. Department of Education, Office of Program Evaluation.

A Compilation of Federal Education Laws. Volume II–Elementary and Secondary Education, Individuals with Disabilities, and Related Programs (1991). Prepared for the Committee on Education and Labor, U.S. House of Representatives, Serial No. 102.K. Washington, D.C.: U.S. Government Printing Office.

Clune, William H. (1992, Spring). "New Answers to Hard Questions Posed by *Rodriguez*: Ending the Separation of School Finance and Educational Policy by Bridging the Gap Between Wrong and Remedy." *Connecticut Law Review*, Vol. 24, No. 3.

Council of Great City Schools (1988). *Teaching and Learning in the Great City Schools.* Washington, D.C.: Council of Great City Schools.

Economic Report of the President, 1993. Council of Economic Advisers. Washington, D.C.: U.S. Government Printing Office.

Eisner, E. (1992, May). "The Federal Reform of Schools: Looking for the Silver Bullet," *Phi Delta Kappan*, pp. 722-723.

ETS, Educational Testing Service (1988).

Ferguson, R. F. (1991, Summer). "Paying for Public Education: New Evidence on How and Why Money Matters." *Harvard Journal on Legislation*, Vol. 28, No. 2.

Finn, J. D., and C. M. Achilles (1990, Fall). "Answers and Questions About Class Size: A Statewide Experiment." *American Educational Research Journal*, Vol. 27, No. 3.

Goertz, M. E., A. Milne, R. J. Coley, M. R. Hoppe, M. J. Gaffney, and D. M. Schember, (1987). *School Districts' Allocation of Chapter 1 Resources*. Princeton, N.J.: Educational Testing Service.

Hanushek, Eric A. (1991, Summer). "When School Finance 'Reform' May Not Be Good Policy." *Harvard Journal on Legislation*, Vol. 28, No. 2.

Hill, P. T. (1992). "Urban Education," *in Urban America: Policy Choices for Los Angeles and the Nation*, J. B. Steinberg, D. W. Lyon, M. E. Vaiana, eds., Santa Monica, Calif.: RAND, MR-100-RC.

Hill, P. T., and J. J. Bonan (1991). *Decentralization and Accountability in Public Education*. Santa Monica, Calif.: RAND, R-4066-MCF/IET.

Hill, P. T., G. E. Foster, and T. Gendler (1990, August). *High Schools with Character*. Santa Monica, Calif.: RAND, R-3944-RC.

Hill, P. T., J. Harvey, and A. Praskac (1993). *Pandora's Box: Accountability and Performance Standards in Vocational Education*. Santa Monica, Calif.: RAND, R-4271-NCRVE/UCB.

Hodgkinson, H. L. (1989). *The Same Client: The Demographics of Education and Service Delivery Systems*. Washington, D.C.: Institute for Educational Leadership.

Johnson, C. M., L. Miranda, A. Sherman, and J. D. Weill (1991). *Child Poverty in America*. Washington, D.C.: Children's Defense Fund.

Kellaghan, Thomas, and George F. Madaus (1993). *National Curricula in European Countries*. Paper prepared for AERA Conference on the National Curriculum, Washington, D.C., June 11, 1993.

Koretz, D. M., G. F. Madaus, E. Haertel, and A. E. Beaton (1992). *National Educational Standards and Testing: A Response to the Recommendations of the National Council on Education Standards and Testing*. Santa Monica, Calif.: RAND, CT-100.

Kozol, J. (1992). *Savage Inequalities: Children in America's Schools*. New York, N.Y.: Harper Perennial.

Madaus, G. F., Maxwell West, M. C. Harmon, R. G. Lomax, and K. A. Viator (1992, October). *The Influence of Testing on Teaching Math and Science in Grades 4-12*. Boston, Mass.: Center for the Study of Testing, Evaluation and Educational Policy.

McClure, P., and R. Martin (1969). *Title I of ESEA: Is It Helping Poor Children?* Washington, D.C.: Washington Research Project of the Southern Center for Studies in Public Policy.

Miller, J. A. (1991). "Chapter 1: An Educational Revolution." *Education Week*, May 22, special insert.

Millsap, M. A., M. Moss, and B. Gamse (1993, February). "Chapter 1 in Public Schools, Draft Final Report." Cambridge, Mass.: Abt Associates.

Millsap, M. A., B. Turnbull, M. Moss, N. Brigham, B. Gamse, and E. Marks (1992). "The Chapter 1 Implementation Study, Interim Report." Washington, D.C.: U.S. Department of Education.

Murnane, Richard J. (1991, Summer). "Interpreting Evidence on 'Does Money Matter?'" *Harvard Journal on Legislation*, Vol. 28, No. 2.

National Center for Education Statistics (1991). *Trends in Academic Progress.* Washington, D.C.: Office of Educational Research, U.S. Department of Education.

———— (1992, June). *The Condition of Education, 1992.* Washington, D.C.: Office of Educational Research, U.S. Department of Education.

———— (1992, October). *Digest of Education Statistics*, 1992. Washington, D.C.: Office of Educational Research, U.S. Department of Education.

National Commission on Excellence in Education (1983). *A Nation at Risk: The Imperative for Educational Reform.* Washington, D.C.: U.S. Department of Education.

NIE, National Institute of Education (1977, September 19). *Administration of Compensatory Education.* Washington, D.C.: U.S. Department of Health, Education and Welfare.

———— (1977, September 30). *The Effects of Services on Student Development.* Washington, D.C.: U.S. Department of Health, Education and Welfare.

Oakes, J. (1990). *Multiplying Inequalities. The Effects of Race, Social Class, and Tracking on Opportunities to Learn Mathematics and Science.* Santa Monica, Calif.: RAND, R-3928-NSF.

Odden, Allan (1990, Summer). "Class Size and Student Achievement: Research-Based Policy Alternatives." *Educational Evaluation and Policy Analysis*, Vol. 12, No. 2.

Pate-Bain, Helen, C. M. Achilles, Jayne Boyd-Zaharias, and Bernard McKenna (1992, November). "Class Size Does Make a Difference." *Phi Delta Kappan*, pp. 253-256.

Rotberg, I. C. (1981). "Federal Policy Issues in Elementary and Secondary Education," *The Federal Role in Education: New Directions for the Eighties*, Robert A. Miller, ed. Washington, D.C.: The Institute for Educational Leadership, Inc.

Shapson, S. M., E. N. Wright, G. Eason, and J. Fitzgerald (1980). "An Experimental Study of the Effects of Class Size." *American Educational Research Journal*, Vol. 17.

Taylor, W., and D. M. Piché (1991). *Shortchanging Children: The Impact of Fiscal Inequity on the Education of Students at Risk.* Report prepared for the Committee on Education and Labor, U.S. House of Representatives, Serial No. 102.O. Washington, D.C.: U.S. Government Printing Office.

U.S. Bureau of the Census (1992, August). *Poverty in the United States: 1991.* Current Population Reports, P-60, No. 181. Washington, D.C.: U.S. Department of Commerce.

U.S. Department of Education (1992, June). *National Assessment of the Chapter 1 Program: The Interim Report.* Washington, D.C.

────── (1993, February). *Reinventing Chapter 1: The Current Chapter 1 Program and New Directions—Final Report of the National Assessment of the Chapter 1 Program.* Washington, D.C.

U.S. House of Representatives (1991). *A Compilation of Federal Education Laws, Volume II —Elementary and Secondary Education, Individuals with Disabilities, and Related Programs.* Committee on Education and Labor, Serial No. 102.K. Washington, D.C.: U.S. Government Printing Office.

Wise, A. Unpublished research. Santa Monica: Calif. RAND.

Wycoff, J. A. (1992, January). "The Intrastate Equality of Public Primary and Secondary Education Resources in the U.S., 1980-1987." *Economics of Education Review*, Vol. 11, No. 1, pp. 19-30.